TRANSNATIONAL LITERATURE

THE BASICS

Paul Jay

Routledge
Taylor & Francis Group

LONDON AND NEW YORK

First published 2021
by Routledge
2 Park Square, Milton Park, Abingdon, Oxon OX14 4RN

and by Routledge
605 Third Avenue, New York, NY 10158

Routledge is an imprint of the Taylor & Francis Group, an informa business

British Library Cataloguing-in-Publication Data
A catalogue record for this book is available from the British Library

Library of Congress Cataloging-in-Publication Data
Names: Jay, Paul, 1946- author.
Title: Transnational literature : the basics / Paul Jay.
Description: Abingdon, Oxon ; New York, NY : Routledge, 2021. |
Series: The basics | Includes bibliographical references and index.
Identifiers: LCCN 2020044666 (print) | LCCN 2020044667 (ebook) |
Subjects: LCSH: Literature and transnationalism.
Classification: LCC PN56.T685 J39 2021 (print) | LCC PN56.T685 (ebook) |
DDC 809/.933582--dc23
LC record available at https://lccn.loc.gov/2020044666
LC ebook record available at https://lccn.loc.gov/2020044667

ISBN: 978-0-367-25226-7 (hbk)
ISBN: 978-0-367-25231-1 (pbk)
ISBN: 978-0-429-28666-7 (ebk)

Typeset in Bembo
by Taylor & Francis Books

For my students.

TRANSNATIONAL LITERATURE

THE BASICS

Transnational Literature: The Basics provides an indispensable overview of this important new field of study and the literature it explores. It concisely describes the various ways in which literature can be understood as being "transnational," explains why scholars in literary studies have become so interested in the topic, and discusses the economic, political, social, and cultural forces that have shaped its development.

The book explores a range of contemporary critical approaches to the subject, highlighting how topics like globalization, cosmopolitanism, diaspora, history, identity, migration, and decolonization are treated by both scholars in the field and the writers they study. The literary works discussed range across the globe and include fiction, poetry, and drama by writers including Jhumpa Lahiri, Chimamanda Ngozi Adichie, Jenny Erpenbeck, Aleksandar Hemon, Viet Thanh Nguyen, Derek Walcott, Louise Bennett, Xiaolu Guo, Sally Wen Mao, Wole Soyinka, and many more. This survey stresses the range and breadth—but also the intersecting interests—of transnational writing, engaging the variety of subjects it covers and emphasizing the range of literary devices (linguistic, formal, narrative, poetic, and dramatic) it employs.

Highlighting the subjects and issues that have become central to fiction in the age of globalization, *Transnational Literature: The Basics* is an essential read for anyone approaching study of this vibrant area.

Paul Jay is Professor Emeritus at Loyola University, Chicago, USA.

The Basics

The Basics is a highly successful series of accessible guidebooks which provide an overview of the fundamental principles of a subject area in a jargon-free and undaunting format.

Intended for students approaching a subject for the first time, the books both introduce the essentials of a subject and provide an ideal springboard for further study. With over 50 titles spanning subjects from artificial intelligence (AI) to women's studies, *The Basics* are an ideal starting point for students seeking to understand a subject area.

Each text comes with recommendations for further study and gradually introduces the complexities and nuances within a subject.

For a full list of titles in this series, please visit www.routledge.com/The-Basics/book-series/B

CONTENTS

PREFACE

I started writing this book in one world, and finished it in another.

I began drafting the early chapters in the spring of 2019. Looking back, it seemed a time of hope, possibly even of renewal. Yes, the value of the humanities as a central pillar of higher education was under attack by a new economic model, one that envisioned a college or university education primarily as vocational training for employment in STEM-dominated fields. From this perspective, the value of a literary education looked particularly suspect. Not just to social commentators and opinion makers, but to students and their parents as well. However, that view was being productively challenged by others who insisted on the enduring value of the humanities. They put particular emphasis on the value of the civic education its disciplines provide, stressing the importance of that education to sustaining healthy democratic institutions. Particularly important for a twenty-first-century education, of course, was the increasingly multicultural and transnational nature of the humanities in general, and of literary studies in particular. For, as we shall see in what follows, the discipline was reorganizing in ways that promised increasing relevance for students entering a dramatically globalizing world in which a sophisticated historical understanding of difference and diversity would be crucial.

At the same time, the production and popularity of fiction, poetry, and drama by an astonishing range of transnational writers was exploding. The old nation-state borders that used to contain and narrow literary writing had dramatically given way under the forces of globalization to a strikingly hybrid, multicultural, cosmopolitan group of writers from places like India, Nigeria, the Caribbean, Asia, and a range of other countries across the Global South. Mobile, well-educated, and savvy about the uses of social media, these writers focused their attention on stories of dispossession and displacement, using the resources of fiction, poetry, and drama to complicate dominant narratives of settlement and progress with complex stories of unsettlement related to colonialism and globalization. For the first time in the history of a world dominated by nation-states, a truly *transnational* literature was not simply emerging. It was becoming a dominant force in the literary marketplace

By April of 2020, when I had completed most of this book in its present form, that world, and the changes that were driving it, came to a dramatic halt. In a matter of a few months the forces of globalization I had been writing about, forces I was treating as economic, cultural, and political, brought us a devastating medical crisis, a global pandemic. As I write, the global spread of the novel coronavirus has resulted in the infection of nearly 32 million people, and the death count is about to reach one million. In an age that has witnessed the globalization of everything, the spread of the novel coronavirus has crippled the global economy, put millions of people out of work, and fundamentally altered the way in which a myriad of institutions, including higher education, do business. It is breathtaking to consider that the entire educational environment operative at the time I started writing this book—along with the economic model that sustained it—has been, at least temporarily, suspended. Simple things we took for granted—small seminars and larger lecture halls packed tight with students eager to engage face-to-face with one another and their professors—have disappeared, replaced by electronic host platforms like Zoom. Students and faculty alike are struggling to create an environment in which they can continue to learn together while family members and friends become sick, and sometimes die, in what has come to seem an unyielding pandemic. Meanwhile, the budgets of colleges and universities are cratering under the loss of tuition funds. Staff and faculty are being furloughed or eliminated. Higher education has come to a kind of standstill, while administrators scramble to plan for a future which, at this point, seems difficult to imagine.

The short-term effects of this crisis on higher education have been devastating, but what will the long-term effects be? At this point it is hard to tell. Whatever they are, they are bound to alter the landscape of higher education for many years to come. A book like this one thrives best in an educational environment based on face-to-face interaction, one in which students read and study texts in an atmosphere of spontaneous, free-form exchange. As I write, that atmosphere has been dramatically disrupted. So too has the world of the arts outside the academy. We have been living in a kind of golden age marked by the increasingly unfettered transnational flow of books, movies, music, and the artists who produce them. Suddenly, whole sectors of the art world have shut down. The pandemic has all but closed down theatrical, operatic, and musical performances, and has radically restricted the screening of films in movie houses. The transnational exchange of artistic productions and shared aesthetic experiences has been abruptly suspended. Of course, literature—its creation, publication, circulation, and reception—has largely been spared this paralysis. Reading is a largely solitary activity, and the global circulation of books does not endanger the health of readers. Author readings are not happening, and book clubs are meeting remotely, but the transnational circulation of literary works seems to be continuing unabated.

However, this does not mean that contemporary transnational literature will not be affected in significant ways by the coronavirus pandemic. One thing seems certain. The pandemic in its myriad guises is going to impact both the subject matter and mood of global fiction, poetry, and drama for years to come. Transnational literature depends, as we shall see, on the *mobility* of transnational writers, and for the time being that mobility is dramatically restricted. Authors, like everyone else, are on lockdown, wearing masks, and carefully practicing social distancing. Surely their experiences are going to become the point of departure for much new contemporary writing, writing that will no doubt be informed by a combination of rage and melancholy that will mark it off from pre-COVID-19 writing. The coronavirus pandemic is a singularly transnational event, and so it is bound in all of its forms—medical, social, cultural, and political—to work its way into the fabric of contemporary transnational literature for quite some time. When I began writing this book, this subject did not exist. As I conclude, it seems destined to play a central role in transnational literature for the foreseeable future. The key subjects in transnational literature explored in this book—mobility, identity, history, borders, migration, globalization, cosmopolitanism—will surely not go away, but they will all be viewed anew through the prism of the pandemic.

*   *   *

This book is truly the culmination of a life's work. I retired from teaching just before beginning to write it, and I have no plans to write another academic book. In the wake of the attacks of 9/11 in 2001, witnessing the hatred, misunderstanding, and xenophobia that erupted in its aftermath, I vowed to direct all of the teaching and research I had left to literature, criticism, and theory that focused on cross-cultural experience and conflict; work that, collectively, sought to illuminate the global history of migration, displacement, border conflicts, and rabid nationalisms, and which explored the history of the nation-state, and of national identity, from the perspective of globalization's long history. That work has now stretched over almost 20 years in the classroom, and through three books, and there are far too many people to thank at this point. This book would not exist without my students, undergraduate and graduate alike, and to them I owe an immense debt. I launched on a journey of learning with them after 9/11, which has never stopped. They taught me as much, if not more, than I taught them. Their enthusiasm for the literature we read together was striking. Many of them had little idea literature could be about their world, and about people like them—Black, Latinx, Asian, South Asian, Queer—the children of immigrants struggling to calibrate their own hybrid identities to an increasingly multicultural, borderless world. A countless number told me they found this experience transformative, and so it was for me as well.

Likewise, my colleagues at Loyola University Chicago, and at various colleges and universities around the country where I was lucky enough to lecture, gave me support and asked hard questions about my ideas that had an indelible impact on my intellectual life, and which gave shape to this book long before I ever conceived of writing it. To my wife, Lynn Woodbury, and my son, Darren Jay, I owe everything. Throughout our lives together we have been a rock-solid family, and that has sustained us all. I love them dearly. In the last year, as I struggled to write this book in the midst of a pandemic which upended our personal lives with dramatic force, they have been wonders of support. Without them I could not have written this book.

Paul Jay
Chicago and Santa Fe, 2020

INTRODUCTION

During the last few decades, both literary production and its study have moved beyond the traditional confines of the nation. Where only a few years ago Western literature seemed monolithic, with its study routinely divided according to national borders, literature written by authors from formerly marginalized or ignored regions of the world, such as Africa, the Caribbean, South Asia, and Latin America, has exploded in popularity, both inside and outside the academy. While literary works have always traveled, and while literature long predates the rise of modern nation states, transnational literature has accelerated dramatically in our age of rapid globalization. However, despite its increasing popularity, the concept of transnational literature still lacks clear definition. Does the phrase mean to call our attention to how specific modes of production, circulation, and reception that cut across the borders of nation-states have shaped literature for centuries, suggesting a model for literary study that views all literature as mobile on a potentially global scale? Or, is transnational literature a kind of literature, emergent at a particular historical moment, engaged with a set of identifiable subjects, and characterized by particular artistic properties? If transnational literature is a kind of literature, is it a contemporary form linked to a particular set of historical forces, or does it have a much longer history? In either case, how can scholars possibly trace the nature, production, circulation, and reception of something called "transnational literature" on a global scale?

Transnational Literature: The Basics provides answers to these questions, and more. It explores the various ways in which literature can be understood as being "transnational," explains why scholars in literary studies have become so interested in the topic, and discusses the economic, political, social, and cultural forces that have shaped both the literature and its study. Since the interests of scholars of transnational literature, and the writers who produce it, are deeply interwoven, the book explores contemporary critical approaches to transnational literature while at the same time surveying a range of fiction, poetry, drama, and creative non-fiction by writers from around the globe. This survey stresses the range and breadth—but also the intersecting interests—of a broad cross-section of writers associated with transnational experience, engaging the variety of subjects it covers and emphasizing the range of literary devices (linguistic, formal, narrative, poetic, and dramatic) it employs.

One of the challenges of approaching transnational literature is that, as we have already indicated, it can be conceptualized in two different ways. One involves understanding that storytelling, poetry, drama, and the literary texts that embody them have always been mobile, and long before there was such a thing as nation-states. From this perspective, the focus is not on transnational literature as a kind of literature with a set of inherent qualities that make it transnational. Rather, it highlights and tracks the transnational patterns of production, circulation, and reception that have enabled certain literary works to transcend the historical and geographical limits of their origins, making them significant in a global way. Transnational literature, from this point of view, is not rooted in any particular historical time period, and there are no particular subjects or formal devices that distinguish it from literature in general. From this perspective, transnational literature comprises texts in any form about any subject that have achieved global and historical importance. As we shall see in more detail in Chapter 2, this approach has led to the resurgence of interest in Goethe's concept of *Weltliteratur*, or world literature, a category that, ultimately, must be distinguished from transnational literature.

Unlike world literature, transnational literature must be understood as a *kind* of literature, emergent at a specific historical moment, linked by a shared set of identifiable subjects, and composed of texts connected by the use of similar literary devices particularly well fitted to explore them. From this perspective, transnational literature is transnational specifically because it emerges at a time when the borders of the modern nation-state have become increasingly porous. This porousness is the product of the twin—and inter-linked—forces of decolonization and globalization, which began in earnest in the first two decades after the Second World War and accelerated in the late twentieth and early twenty-first centuries. These forces led to the proliferation of literary works produced by writers from regions of the world formerly colonized, and largely denigrated, by the West. Combined with the forces of economic and cultural globalization, decolonization both produced and made available to a global audience literary works by an increas-ingly mobile group of writers from places such as Nigeria and Zambia to the Dominican Republic, Bosnia, and Pakistan. These works are linked both by the historical circumstances of their production, and by their shared exploration of subjects that deal specifically with transnational experience—with migration, dis-placement, exile, border crossings, cosmopolitanism, globalization, and the forms of personal and cultural hybridity these forces have produced. Seen this way, transnational literature—understood as a *kind* of contemporary literature—can be thought of as transnational in two specific ways: its geographical scope represents a dramatic, his-torically specific expansion of literary production (especially in the Global South), and the subjects it treats are particularly associated with transnational experiences—personal, social, cultural, and political—spurred by the forces of decolonization and globalization.

Taken together, the overlapping categories of world and transna-tional literature have shifted the geographical and cultural organiza-tion of literary studies in two important ways. They have focused attention on the transnational aspects of literature's production, cir-culation, and reception, while at the same time fostering new interest in literary works from formerly marginalized or ignored regions of the world, many of which are about cross-cultural or transnational experience (here the emergence of both multiculturalism and border studies in the last decades of the twentieth century proved particularly important, as we shall see). It is important to note that the transna-tional turn in literary studies has its roots in political, economic, social, and cultural changes that began outside academia. For example, the collapse of institutionalized Western imperial domination of whole regions of Africa, the Caribbean, and South Asia in the years after the Second World War led to the independence of formerly colonized countries, which in turn fed immigration from those countries to metropolitan centers in the West. As globalization accelerated during this period, nation-state borders became increasingly permeable. The mobility of commerce, people, and cultural practices rapidly increased, both in Europe and the United States, where the 1965 Immigration and Nationalization Act offered the possibility of immigration to those formerly barred, from places like South Asia and Latin America. As a result of all these changes, the demographic constitution of Western nations began to change dramatically, and, perhaps more importantly for the contemporary development of literary studies, the population of students in humanities courses became increasingly diverse and international. At the same time, the production of literature by formerly marginalized and suppressed populations exploded in popularity among general readers. Writers themselves became part of a new and increasingly mobile literary transnationalism (including not only those from formerly colonized countries, but others from countries behind the former "Iron Curtain" dominated by the Soviet Union). Like nearly everything else, literature became a global commodity that, in the age of the Internet, began to cross nation-state borders with increasing ease. Literature written in English, either from locations outside of Britain and the United States, or inside those countries by immigrant or refugee writers displaced by the forces of globalization, began to enter the global literary marketplace, and translated works from all over the globe accelerated in circulation.

Given the reciprocal relationship between the scholarly and critical fields of world literature and transnational literature, on the one hand, and the contemporary explosion of transnational literature itself, on the other, this book explores the rise of transnational literature as *both* a field of study and a kind of literature, stressing throughout the symbiotic relationship between the two. Part I begins with a discussion, in Chapter 1, of the meaning of the terms transnational and transnationalism, exploring how they are conceptualized generally, and how they are related to the idea of the nation and the ideal of cosmopolitanism. Chapter 2 focuses more specifically on the historical development of disciplinary approaches to studying literature in a global or transnational context, including comparative, postcolonial, border, globalization, and diaspora studies. Chapter 3 takes as its point of departure the distinction between *studying* literature in a transnational context, where the emphasis is on histories of production and circulation ("world literature" is the dominant model here), and conceiving of transnational literature as a *kind* of literature, emergent at a specific historical moment and characterized by an intersecting set of subjects broadly informed by the forces of decolonization and globalization. This definition of transnational literature forms the context for our discussion of the broad selection of transnational literary works in Part II.

While Part I focuses on the rise of transnational literature as a scholarly field of study, and explores different critical and theoretical frameworks for its study, Part II turns its attention to a discussion of representative works of transnational literature across the genres of fiction, poetry, drama, and creative non-fiction. Chapters 4, 5, 6, 7, and 8 demonstrate a range of ways to read transnational literature, and are organized around a linked set of general topics—mobility, borders, migration, identity, and history, respectively—which together provide the context for both a broad thematic overview of transnational literature and an examination of the range of stylistic, literary, and narrative devices used by transnational writers. Finally, Chapter 9 explores transnational drama or theater as both a written and performative medium. It will become clear as this book unfolds that the concerns of literary scholars who study transnational literature overlap with the concerns of those who write it; a fact that dramatizes the symbiotic relationship between the literary analysis of transnational literature and the literature itself.

PART I

CONCEPTUALIZING TRANSNATIONAL LITERATURE

THE NATION AND BEYOND

TRANSNATIONAL

The term "transnational" is a relatively new one. According to *The Oxford English Dictionary* (http://www.oed.com), its usage dates from the second decade of the twentieth century. In general, the term means "extending or having interests extending beyond national bounds or frontiers." It is important to underscore the fact that "transnational" is an adjective. That is, it is a modifying term. There is no such thing as transnational. Rather, the term refers to anything that can be thought of as having a transnational range, dimension, or character (companies, organizations, films, literary works, etc.). Transnational gets its main meaning from the prefix "trans," which means "across, through, over, to or on the other side of, beyond, outside of, from one place, person, thing, or state to another." The prefix trans also implies the action of being "beyond, surpassing," and "transcending." It is also worth pointing out that "transgress" bears a relationship to the verb form of trans, as used in *transgredi*, which means to step across—and, *transgressio*, which refers to going over or transgressing the law.

This last point is important because transnational perspectives are often transgressive in the sense that they either challenge or contest altogether notions of purity and exclusivity often associated with nationalism. A transnational perspective shifts primary attention from the universal to the particular. Its concern is less with what is central than with what is thought of or treated as marginal. It is as interested in what makes people different as it is in what seems to make them the same. Where British, German, or Spanish literary studies may be primarily interested in how literary works express or shape forms of ethnic, racial, and cultural belonging that reflect a national character, focusing on literature from a transnational perspective orients the reader toward the other and focuses attention on understanding difference. And, while the study of national literatures understandably operates within the fixed borders of the nation-state, from a transnational perspective borders are understood as historically and existentially porous. For this reason, a transnational approach to literature starts from the premise that individual subjectivity is always *intersubjectivity*. That is, while it may be shaped by forces within the nation, those forces often have their origins outside it. This means that cultures and identities are never singular and pure. They are hybrid and syncretic. Understood from this point of view, a transnational perspective usually understands identity and culture in dialectical terms. As the critic Laura Doyle puts it in "Toward a Philosophy of Transnationalism" (2009), "the power of transnational studies lies in its fundamentally dialectical approach," an approach that "opens the way to a fresh consideration of the human or existential subject of history" understood not only in terms of "the movements of people and capital across national borders" but also as "other-oriented interactions between and among nations, making them mutually shaping and mutually contingent."

To think of literature from a transnational perspective is to put an emphasis on transit—on mobility, migration, travel, and exchange, forms of experience that create bonds between people that, while fostering a sense of national unity, also connect people and their cultural practices across, over, and through geographic and human-made borders. However, we need to keep in mind that transnational forces also interact within the borders of a nation, that identities and cultural practices within nations are always forming and reforming across the differences we associate with race, ethnicity, religion, gender, and nation. In effect, transnational spaces form a kind of crossroads, whether they intersect through very different cultural geographies, as was the case, for example, with the Silk Road, or whether they occur within the territory of a nation-state.

A transnational perspective also insists that we think critically about concepts like universality, purity, and homogeneity, especially when those concepts derive from a specifically Western perspective.

One example is Kwame Appiah's insistence in *Cosmopolitanism: Ethics in a World of Strangers* (2006) that what we think of as national cultures are in fact the product of contamination by other cultures. He discounts the idea, for example, that forms of transnational exchange destroy cultural authenticity. Instead, he points out that cultures are always in flux, evolving through forms of cross-pollination that render the "authentic" fluid and changeable. From such a perspective, any strict distinction between purity and contamination is a fiction. And, Appiah points out, these processes are not new, a recent product of contemporary forms of globalization. In fact, they have a long history, one that has always shaped identities and cultures across national borders. As Homi K. Bhabha put it in *The Location of Culture* (1994), "the very concepts of homogenous national cultures, the consensual or contiguous transmission of historical traditions, or 'organic' ethnic communities—as the grounds of cultural comparativism—are in a profound process of redefinition."

The term transnational*ism* is often invoked casually in discussions of transnational formations, be they political, cultural, or artistic. However, transnationalism carries with it some specific implications that distinguish it from the term transnational. While transnational suggests a set of relations and so usually refers to a condition, transnationalism implies a doctrine, and suggests either advocacy or rejection of something transnational. The distinction between the two terms, of course, turns on the *ism* in transnationalism. Feminine means one thing, feminism quite another. Like feminism, transnationalism implies some kind of doctrine, ideology, or politics that can be advocated or rejected. Critics differ on whether transnationalism is a destructive force because it encourages cultural homogenization and produces uneven economic effects, or whether it is a liberating force that enables new and resistant forms of subjectivity and syncretic cultural practices, that counter the negative forces of nationalism. For some, transnationalism suggests a set of humanitarian ideals advocating diversity, openness, inclusiveness, cooperation, and social justice. For others, however, it is associated with a set of economic and cultural practices linked to globalization that threaten the autonomy and integrity of nations and the ideals upon which they are founded.

Advocating transnationalism, finally, also runs the risk of marginalizing the local and the particular. From this point of view, transnationalism is, as the American critic Kenneth Burke put it in *Permanence and Change: An Anatomy of Purpose* (1936), a way of seeing which can, paradoxically, become a way of *not* seeing. Paying attention to the transnational scope of literature, film, or any other cultural phenomenon has a real value, but it can distract us from the importance of understanding the local, particular roots of a social or cultural phenomenon. The best approach in this context is, again, a dialectical one: tracking the historically complex interaction of local, regional, national, and transnational forces in the production of everything from individual subjectivity to belief systems, ideological formations, and literary production. For, in the final analysis, the relationship between the local and the global is symbiotic. Transnational forces of every kind flow across localities, but they are absorbed by those localities in quite different ways that disrupt and mutate them as they continue to move through other places.

NATION

With this broad understanding of the term transnational in mind, then, thinking of literature in transnational terms requires exploring its origins and circulation in modes of production that extend beyond the nation, and the racial, ethnic, and religious groups that comprise it. From this perspective, it is important to note, the organizing of literary studies by nation looks rather arbitrary. It reflects the nineteenth- and twentieth-century consolidation of nation-states more than something that is intrinsic to literature itself. However, it is also the case that there can be no transnational literature without the concept of the nation, since nothing can be understood as transcending—or seeking to exceed or cut across— the nation without our having some grasp of the concept of the nation in the first place. This is no simple matter, however, since the term nation is both complicated and multifaceted. The *Online Etymology Dictionary* (https://www.etymonline.com/word/nation) notes that the word derives from the Old French *nacion*, which means "birth, rank; descendants, relatives; country, homeland (12c.)," and also "from Latin nationem (nominative natio) 'birth, origin; breed, stock, kind, species; race of people, tribe,' literally 'that which has been born,'" with "derivatives referring to procreation and familial and tribal groups." As this etymology indicates, a nation can be defined in terms of birth, rank, descent, breed, species, cultural practices, and race; any seemingly inherent characteristic a group of people believe indicate they belong to the same genus.

It is important to note that there are key differences between nations and states. Nations are not necessarily states, as the etymology above indicates, since it makes no reference to either geographical or legal boundaries. Some nations are stateless, and some states are made up of more than one nation. While a nation is largely a cultural category, a state is a legal entity. According to the *Oxford English Dictionary (OED)*, a state is "a community of people living in a defined territory and government; a commonwealth, a nation," or "the territory occupied by such a community." A nation, although conflated in this definition with the state, is more a product of the imagination than the law, hence Benedict Anderson's characterization of nations as "imagined communities" (in *Imagined Communities: Reflections on the Origin and Spread of Nationalism*, 1986), a phrase that stresses how a nation is shaped around socially constructed ideals, imagined by the community it names as sharing a set of shared characteristics, beliefs, and practices.

One way to think about the difference between considering the nation as a cultural entity, and thinking of it as a legal one, is to recognize that the cultural ideal of the nation is based on a set of ostensibly intrinsic qualities like "blood," "race," "ethnicity," and language, while the idea of the nation as a state is based on purely extrinsic criteria, that is, the law. An intrinsic approach to national belonging is based on qualities that are supposedly inherent and immutable (and of course, often highly subjective), while an extrinsic one is based on largely objective legal criteria. Another way of thinking about this difference is in the context of the terms *ethnic* and *civic*. An ethnic approach to the nation is largely consistent with the idea that a nation is defined by intrinsic or inherent qualities shared by a an ethnic group, a race, or a tribe, while a civic approach to the nation envisions national belonging as rooted in the legal responsibilities that come with citizenship.

The approach to national belonging associated with the idea that the nation is based on a set of intrinsic characteristics people are born with often translates into a quasi-metaphysical conception of the nation. These are characteristics you either have by birth, or you don't. For this reason, appeals to nationalism often traffic in idealist rhetoric about the blood of the nation, or the spirit or soul of the folk who make it up, rhetoric which sees national identity in homogenous terms. In the extreme, it can lead, of course, to virulent, dangerous, and even genocidal forms of nationalism. An extrinsic or civic approach to national belonging, on the other hand, understands the nation as a legal entity in which people of different races and ethnicities, and with very different languages, religious beliefs, and cultural practices form a national ideal based on heterogeneity and a commitment to equal justice under the law.

These differences call attention to the fact that the nation is less an objective than a political entity. This is obviously the case with regard to the conception of the nation as an essentially civic or legal entity, in which the rights and responsibilities of individual members are worked out and regulated by the state through a political process that shapes legally binding statutes. However, the cultural or ethnic concept of the nation is equally political, as it uses essentialist language about blood, race, and cultural practices to conceptualize the nation in ways that exercise power and therefore have political consequences. In either form, the nation has to be understood not as a purely descriptive category, but as something that shapes and regulates the identity and the behavior both of people deemed to belong to it, and those who are excluded from it. This shaping and regulating is perhaps most dramatically apparent in the educational systems nation-states develop, but it also takes place in religious and cultural institutions, including the media. National sovereignty plays a role, then, in shaping personal identity, and allegiance to the nation involves a level of subservience not just to its laws but to its ideals. This is one of the reasons why the term *subjectivity* has come to replace the term *identity* in discussions of the individual, since it is increasingly clear that individuality is not simply a state of freedom and autonomy in which inherent characteristics define individuals, but that individuals are subject to—and therefore subjects of—the legal, religious, cultural, and political discourses that shape them.

Since identity with respect to national belonging is defined by citizenship, it is important to note the pressure both globalization and transnationalism have put on the idea of citizenship. The term "citizen," according to the *OED*, originated in the fourteenth century as a reference to the inhabitants of a city or town who had specific legal rights or privileges. Once states came into existence as legal entities, the term citizen came to refer as well to the inhabitants of those states and the legal rights and privileges that came with citizenship within them. To the extent the state became conflated with the nation, citizenship was then extended to the idea of national belonging, and the responsibilities and rights that come with it. Economic and cultural globalization, of course, have extended the parameters of citizenship even further to include the idea of global (or, for our purposes, transnational) citizenship. All of the forces associated with globalization we mentioned earlier have produced an extraordinary capacity for personal and mass mobility. Combined populations of immigrants and refugees have flowed out of their home countries and taken up residence (legally and illegally) in other countries. Here, as Rainer Bauböck has pointed out in "Stakeholder Citizenship: An Idea Whose Time Has Come?" (2008), we run up against a practical paradox:

> Democracy is government accountable to its citizens, and states are territorial jurisdictions. International migration creates a tension between these two basic facts about our world because it produces citizens living outside the country whose government is supposed to be accountable to them and inside a country whose government is not accountable to them. The result is a mismatch between citizenship and the territorial scope of legitimate political authority.

As Bauböck notes, the increasingly transnational flow of people in an age of rapid globalization creates so much heterogeneity among national populations that the very idea of national citizenship turns into a kind of quandary. This is because the ideal of the nation as a relatively single and cohesive ethnic, racial, religious, linguistic, and cultural entity has increasingly given way, in the wake of decolonization, migration, globalization, and the ease of travel, to the creation of multi-ethnic, religious, racial, linguistic, and cultural populations within nations that formerly thought of themselves as singular and cohesive. As we shall see, the concept of the nation, and the pressures put on national belonging and national identity by these combined forces, have been a major topic in transnational literature. Much of it features explorations of identity and belonging in the context of empire, colonization, nation-building, technology, and globalization. This exploration deals with intersecting historical, political, cultural, social, and personal forces.

COSMOPOLITANISM

One important facet of this engagement, both in transnational literature and among critics who have studied it from various angles, is a fascination with *cosmopolitanism*. Understood in its positive sense as embracing inclusiveness and difference, rejecting parochialism, and overcoming prejudices often associated with nationalism, the advocacy of cosmopolitanism is closely associated with the advocacy of transnationalism, and has often been associated with a sense of global citizenship. For, like transnationalism, cosmopolitanism embraces worldliness and a sense of global belonging, comfort with otherness and difference, and a concern that narrow forms of nationalism inevitably divide people from one another, and worse, help to fuel xenophobia. Cosmopolitanism is also consistent with the idea that culture is inherently hybrid and syncretic, and is associated with a political point of view that seeks to value both national sovereignty *and* human rights. From this point of view, cosmopolitanism has emerged in our own time as an ethical or moral imperative. As Kwame Anthony Appiah puts it in *Cosmopolitanism*, to be cosmopolitan is to see oneself as a citizen not just of a nation but of the world. This means that we have "obligations to others, obligations that stretch beyond those to whom we are related by the ties of kith and kind, or even the more formal ties of a shared citizenship" (xv).

This view of cosmopolitanism has deep roots in the West running all the way back to the Greek philosopher, Diogenes, who proclaimed in the fourth century BCE that he was a *kosmopolites*, that is, a citizen of the world. The idea of being cosmopolitan was taken up with greater force in the third century CE by the Stoics, who understood citizenship as a commitment to human beings per se rather than to a narrow political entity. Taken up later by the Romans, Stoic cosmopolitanism became associated both with conquest and empire under Alexander the Great, and with a Christian ideal of human inter-connectedness. However, as Appiah makes clear, cosmopolitanism did not emerge as a philosophical ideal until the Enlightenment, when the concept of world citizenship came to inform points of view like Goethe's in the conceptualization of *Weltliteratur*. At this point, cosmopolitanism became associated with the idea there was such a thing as "the human condition" shared as something universal, but also with a kind of worldly sophistication connected to urban life and travel. Cosmopolitanism inevitably became entangled with both colonialism and capitalism as the two spread globally, so much so that Marx and Engels came to associate cosmopolitanism with global capitalism.

From this point on, cosmopolitanism became a controversial concept. While, on the one hand, it is associated with an embrace of the worldly over the narrowly parochial, and with an openness to the idea that all humans are connected to one another in ways that transcend nation-state borders, on the other hand it has also been associated with empire, colonialism, and the negative effects of economic globalization. Critics skeptical of the term have often pointed out that cosmopolitanism has been historically associated with class privilege and what is often a colonizing perspective. For example, Walter Mignolo, concerned that cosmopolitanism has too often been closely linked to a kind of smug superiority in the West underscored by its association with a voyeuristic interest in otherness, Mignolo calls for a "critical cosmopolitanism" rooted in non-Western perspectives, one that is grounded in what he calls "colonial difference" ("The Many Faces of Cosmo-Polis: Border Thinking and Critical Cosmopolitanism," 2000). According to Mignolo, a critical cosmopolitanism must develop from formerly "silenced and marginalized voices … bringing themselves into the conversation" about cosmopolitanism a conversation that ought to take place across borders, so that what he calls "border thinking" can transform cosmopolitanism from a subaltern perspective (735–6). Likewise, Enrique Dussel, another critic wary of the negative baggage the term cosmopolitanism carries, worries that its link to a Eurocentric modernity make it inappropriate as a unifying force in the transnationalizing of literary and cultural studies ("World-System and 'Trans'-Modernity," 2002).

More recent discussions of the relationship between the terms transnational and cosmopolitan continue to pursue this debate. In their editorial introduction to *Locating Transnational Ideals* (2010), for example, Walter Goebel and Saskia Schabio point out that many of the essays they have collected are skeptical of a "transnational euphoria" prompted "by a vision of the utopian communicative potential of new media like the internet" (2). They associate this euphoria with a kind of global neo-liberalism often endorsed by those who uncritically praise transnationalism and cosmopolitanism. In their view, versions of the cosmopolitan like Mignolo's that are "the product of intensive intercultural dialogues *and* economic/political/legal strife" are preferable to the naive forms of euphoria they associate with neo-liberalism (2). Along with their contributors, they endorse what Paul Gilroy calls a cosmopolitanism "from below" (5). The positions Mignolo and Gilroy take on cosmopolitanism are also echoed by Françoise Lionnet and Shu-mei Shih in their introduction to the essays collected in *Minor Transnationalism* (2005). The "minor" in their title marks the importance of a form of worldliness or anti-parochialism similar to the kind invoked by Mignolo and Gilroy, a worldliness that resists colonialist perspectives and has its roots in formerly colonized, ignored, or subaltern, regions. For Lionnet and Shih, a minor transnationalism decenters the West in order to develop "lateral" connections between minority or subaltern cultures. In so doing, they insist, "the transnational can … be conceived as a space of exchange and participation wherever processes of hybridization occur and where it is still possible for cultures to be produced and performed without necessary mediation by the center" (5).

Not surprisingly, these arguments about cosmopolitanism work their way into many transnational literary texts. As we shall see later, in Amitav Ghosh's *Hungry Tide* (2004), two characters are associated with a cosmopolitan point of view that is contrasted with village life in the Sunderbans and challenged by their time there. We will also see that cosmopolitan elites are front and center in Nadine Gordimer's novel, *The Pickup* (2001), both in the guise of urban liberals and white suburban economic elites in contemporary Johannesburg, South Africa. They figure prominently in the main character's sense of alienation from the cultural and political world she has grown up in. Cosmopolitanism is treated most explicitly as a philosophical ideal and a political problem in Teju Cole's *Open City* (2011), where it is associated as well with the worldly ideal of the flâneur. Julius, the narrator, embodies the point of view of the cosmopolitan flâneur in the initial sections of the book set in New York City, but the term's problematical implications come into the foreground when Julius travels to Belgium and becomes involved with two migrants from North Africa, Farouq and Khalid. The three of them, as we shall see in our discussion of the novel, argue at length over the pros and cons of a cosmopolitan perspective, and, when Julius returns home he sends a copy of Appiah's book on cosmopolitanism to Khalid.

FURTHER READING

Anderson, Benedict. *Imagined Communities: Reflections on the Origin and Spread of Nationalism* (London: Verso, 1983).

Appiah, Kwame Anthony. *Cosmopolitanism: Ethics in a World of Strangers* (New York: W.W. Norton and Company, 2006).

Bhabha, Homi K. *The Location of Culture* (London: Routledge, 1994).

Green, Nancy L. *The Limits of Transnationalism* (Chicago: University of Chicago Press, 2019).

Mignolo, Walter. *Local Histories/Global Designs: Coloniality, Subaltern Knowledges, and Border Thinking* (Princeton: Princeton University Press, 2000).

REFERENCES

Anderson, Benedict. *Imagined Communities: Reflections on the Origin and Spread of Nationalism* (London: Verso, 1983).

Appiah, Kwame Anthony, *Cosmopolitanism: Ethics in a World of Strangers* (New York: W.W. Norton, 2006).

Bauböck, Rainer. "Stakeholder Citizenship: An Idea Whose Time Has Come?" (2008). Retrieved from https://www.migrationpolicy.org/research/stakeholder-citizenship-idea-whose-time-has-come.

Bhabha, Homi K. *The Location of Culture* (New York: Routledge, 1994).

Burke, Kenneth. *Permanence and Change: An Anatomy of Purpose* (Berkeley and Los Angeles: University of California Press, 1954 [1936]).

Cole, Teju. *Open City* (New York: Random House, 2011).

Doyle, Laura. "Toward a Philosophy of Transnationalism," in *Journal of Transnational Studies*, 1 (1), 2009. Retrieved from https://escholarship.org/uc/item/9vr1k8hk.

Dussel, Enrique. "World-System and 'Trans'-Modernity," in *Nepantla: Views from South*, 3 (2), 2002, 221–244.

Goebel, Walter, and Saskia Schabio, eds. *Locating Transnational Ideals* (New York: Routledge, 2010).

Ghosh, Amitav. *Hungry Tide* (New York: Harper Collins, 2004).

Gordimer, Nadine. *The Pickup* (New York: Viking, 2001).

Lionnet, Françoise, and Shu-mei Shih, eds. *Minor Transnationalism* (Durham and London: Duke University Press, 2005).

Mignolo, Walter. "The Many Faces of Cosmo-Polis: Border Thinking and Critical Cosmopolitanism," in *Public Culture*, 2000, 12 (3), 721–748.

TRANSNATIONALIZING
LITERARY STUDIES

Transnational literary studies, as we have already noted, are characterized by a kind of conglomeration of subfields including multicultural, world, postcolonial, diasporic, and border literatures. It is important to keep in mind, however, that literary works do not naturally occur within such categories. Terms like "multicultural literature," "postcolonial literature," "diasporic literature," "world literature," and "border literature" are the creation of literary scholars and critics. They are historically specific categories used to organize literary study that develop, change, come into prominence, and sometimes fall into disuse over time. They are used to provide order to the study of literary works after they are produced, but do not necessarily refer to properties inherent to the works themselves.

This means that such categories are, to a large degree, both arbitrary and contingent. We are used to making generic distinctions, for example, between fiction, poetry, drama, and non-fiction, to categorize literary works by historical periods (Medieval, Renaissance, early modern, Romantic, Victorian, Modern, Postmodern, etc.), to divide the study of literature by nation (British, American, French, Spanish, German, Japanese, Russian, Chinese, or South African, etc.), or, more recently, with respect to gender, sexuality, race, ethnicity, and ability (feminist literature, queer literature, African-American literature, disability studies, and so forth). In fact, in each of these instances, these categorical distinctions overlap and blur. Fiction uses poetic language and even some of its forms; poetry can be prosaic and take narrative forms; drama can be poetic or prosaic, fictional or historical; non-fiction can employ forms of narrative emplotment; fiction can incorporate historical fact, and authors can have multiple national identities.

Moreover, the historical periods we have traditionally used to organize literary study and categorize literary works are also arbitrary and fluid. For example, there was no such thing as "Medieval" or "Renaissance" literature when works we characterize as Medieval or Renaissance literature were written. Both the time periods and the characteristics of "Romantic," "Victorian," and "Modern" literature were often determined well after the publication of works associated with them. The same point holds for the category of national literatures. We often assume that they have a set of stylistic characteristics or shared subjects that makes them cohere, that Indian, Portuguese, British, or Italian literature is about *being* Indian, Portuguese, British, or Italian; indeed, that the purpose of national literatures is in part to express or represent national identity. However, more often than not, it is scholars rather than literary writers who pursue this idea as they read and analyze literary works with an eye toward what they might tell us about national identity. And finally, while many writers of African, Hispanic, Asian, or indigenous descent embrace these labels, many others resist them, not wanting to be reduced as a writer to either a single or hyphenated identity category. The same holds for women writers who often chafe against being labeled as "women" or even "feminist" writers. These categories, too, while they seem important, even urgent in our own time, have less to do with the nature of individual works (or their authors) and more to do with the identities writers and critics want to foreground at a particular historical moment.

The point here is not that such categories are useless, but rather that there is a reciprocal relationship between *kinds* of literary works, and the scholarly and critical vocabularies we use to study them. Like any category that seems to name a kind of literature, transnational literature is in fact a fluid and somewhat arbitrary category born of the interaction between historical change, literary writing, and academic study. It has emerged in recent decades as a kind of catch-all term for literature with some kind of global scope that defies categorization with regard to its national origins, and has been born out of the convergence of specific historical developments over the course of the twentieth and twenty-first centuries.

For this reason, transnational literature and transnational literary *studies* share a fluid border. They have a reciprocal and co-constitutive relationship. What counts as transnational literature is constantly—and simultaneously—being worked out among writers, reviewers, and readers in the public sphere, and by critics and scholars in the academy. Scholars, critics, and theorists, of course, read, study, and research the literature they write about, but writers also read, study, and research the work of scholars, critics, and theorists. For this reason, there is often a clear overlap between the issues transnational fiction writers, poets, and dramatists engage and those that critics and theorists explore. In texts like Teju Cole's novel, *Open City*, for example, that relationship is clearly a kind of circular one in which issues treated by a range of critics and theorists, from (in Cole's case) Walter Benjamin and Edward Said to Benedict Anderson and Kwame Anthony Appiah, get woven into the novel both because its characters have been reading them, and because the issues they write about are central to what the novel is attempting to explore.

While we have had occasion to reference a range of new approaches to the study of literature in a transnational context, there are four key programmatic formations that deserve particular attention given the important historical role they have played in fostering transnational approaches to literary study: Comparative Literature, Postcolonial Studies, Border Studies, and Globalization Studies. What follows is a brief overview of each of these approaches, one that stresses their historical development and their intersectionality, but which also strives to underscore important differences between them.

COMPARATIVE LITERATURE

The first scholarly field to take a transnational approach to the study of literature was comparative literature. Originating in the early nineteenth century, comparative literature had developed into a full-fledged academic field by the end of the century. As its name implies, the field did not limit itself to the study of a single national literature, but instead focused on the influences national literatures have had on one another, with the ultimate aim of developing a comparative history of literature. While, on the surface, comparative literature seems to shift scholarly attention away from the nation-state model, in actuality it has nearly always relied on that model as its major organizing principle. This is one of the things that distinguishes comparative literature from the new field of transnational literature. Comparative literature is a multinational, but not a transnational, approach to literary study. As such, it has had the effect of broadening the geographical scope of literary study while at the same time reinforcing the centrality of the nation in literary studies. This problem was compounded by its historical Eurocentricity; for the bedrock of comparative literature until late in the twentieth century, as Jan M. Ziolkowski has observed, had always been European literatures ("Incomparable: The Destiny of Comparative Literature, Globalization or Not," 2007), a tendency concisely glossed by Dipesh Chakrabarry as "first in Europe, then elsewhere" (*Provincializing Europe: Postcolonial Thought and Historical Difference*, 2000, 6). The orientation of its scholarship reflects the fact that comparative literature studies originated, took root, and prospered first in the United States and Europe.

From its beginnings scholars were divided about what the orientation of comparative literature ought to be. Some, like the great Italian critic, Benedetto Croce, insisted that comparing literary themes in literature was an "arid" enterprise, and that the field ought to focus on producing a "comparative history of literature" (quoted in Ziolkowski, 22). Others, like Rene Wellek, disagreed, insisting that "the study of all literature from an international perspective" should foster "a consciousness of the unity of all creation and experience" (quoted in Ziolkowski, 23). Where Croce wants comparative literature to embrace a quasi-empirical approach in constructing a vast literary history, Wellek takes a phenomenological approach, based as it is on the idea that humans share a kind of metaphysical "unity," and that the study of literature can tell us something about the universality of human creation and experience.

The difference between transnational and comparative literature as fields of study is rooted in the different meanings of "compare" and "trans." Comparison is interested in two objects thought of as having a coherence, unity, or set of boundaries, like those of the nation-states or national literatures that are the point of departure for comparison. Comparative literature therefore has a kind of binary structure eschewed by scholars working on literature from a transnational perspective, where the focus is on interactivity, mobility, fluidity, and shape-shifting, on what happens when ideas, and literary styles and subjects, move across, through, and beyond the kinds of borders that demarcate the zones of comparative literature. As Ziolkowski puts it, the "supranationalism" of comparative literature "cannot be lightly readjusted to fit transnationalism" (16). This is largely because comparative literature is the product of a historical moment very different from our own, one in which the idea of the nation-state solidified in the context of a sense of Western exceptionalism so pronounced that the very ideas of universality and civilization became associated with it. Operating under the auspices of this "supranationalism," comparative literature became increasingly problematic in the decades after the Second World War when both decolonization and globalization became the new dominant historical forces. Writing in 2012, Ziolkowski saw the implication of these changes for comparative literature quite clearly. The forces of globalization, he writes, have fostered "a greater connectedness, interdependence, and integration of economies, politics, technologies, and cultures," changes that, collectively, "could lead to the gradual erasure of national identities and boundaries that could be argued to have underlain the conception of comparative literature, especially since the Second World War" (29). "Such transnationalism," he continues, is marked by "increased interconnections between people throughout the world and relaxed boundaries between nations," all of which allows for "greater freedom of self-expression," both for "nationless ethnic groups" and the kinds of mobile, displaced writers associated with transnational literature.

In the face of these recent historical changes, comparative literature has done much to adjust its orientation, paying increasing attention to non-Western literature, the literature of the global South, to literature engaged with popular culture, and to texts produced on the margins of nation-states, in diaspora communities and among writers who do not identify with a single nation and therefore usefully complicate the models of comparison that have traditionally characterized work in comparative literature. For this reason, the lines of demarcation between comparative literature, postcolonial, global, border, and diaspora studies have become increasingly—and productively—blurrier. The sections that follow explore these changes in more detail.

POSTCOLONIAL STUDIES

By pushing back against its historical Eurocentrism, postcolonial studies helped to dramatically expand the field of comparison opened by comparative literary studies. It also served to transform the historical, political, and ideological perspectives of the field. Where comparative literary studies were broadly interested in a range of intersections between canonical literary works from around the globe that called attention to the universality of human experience, and while it operated with a set of aesthetic criteria largely inherited from Matthew Arnold—a commitment to focus on what he famously asserted was simply the "best that had been thought and said" (*Culture and Anarchy*, 1869)—postcolonial studies operated from a decidedly different set of premises. First of all, it situated the study of literature both by Western and non-Western writers within the framework of empire, colonialism, and decolonization. This provided a new historical context for the study of literature that called attention to the political, economic, and ideological bases of what were supposedly disinterested and purely literary or aesthetic judgements about what constituted literature and its greatness. This postcolonial perspective helped to usher in a range of work on the history of canon formation that challenged—and constructively complicated—much of the criteria that went into the construction of not only national literary canons, but formed as well the foundation for both world and comparative literary studies.

The decidedly interdisciplinary orientation of postcolonial studies also helped to transform work being done in comparative literature. Indeed, by the first decade of the twenty-first century the fields of comparative literature, postcolonial literature, and globalization studies had begun to merge and overlap. Drawing on a range of disciplines including history, political science, philosophy, linguistics, and sociology, postcolonial studies helped facilitate a dramatic expansion both of the subjects covered in comparative literature and the canon of texts it tended to work with, supplementing the reading of canonical Western texts with an increasingly diverse and transnational set of works from formerly ignored or marginalized parts of the globe. In so doing, postcolonial literary studies provided a useful template for transnational studies, calling attention to and providing a historical context for understanding the transnational nature of literary production, and supplying both a critical vocabulary and set of new methodologies for its study. While, as we shall see a bit later, there are clear distinctions to be made between "postcolonial" and "transnational" literature, it is important to recognize that a postcolonial perspective calls attention to one of the fundamental paradoxes inherent in the rise of transnational literature: the central role that colonialism has played in its development. On the one hand, the violent conquest of the Americas, much of Africa, and nearly all of South Asia by European powers like Spain, Portugal, and Britain, left devastation and ruin everywhere. Indigenous populations in all of these places died in massive numbers through warfare, disease, and starvation. Africans were brought in chains to the Americas and forced to work as slaves, followed by indentured servants from South Asia. Indigenous religious and cultural practices in the Americas, Africa, and across the globe—along with the artistic, storytelling, and expressive practices attached to them—were systematically exterminated, replaced by Western religious and cultural narratives. The whole way of life of people across the globe was decimated by the suppression of cultural systems, be they Aztec, Igbo, Hindu, or Islamic, replaced by Western religious and educational systems that set out to methodically transform colonized peoples into Westernized subjects.

And yet, these systematic forms of brutalization had a secondary, and deeply ironic effect. As the conquered, the colonized, and the enslaved were forced to incorporate the religious and cultural worlds of their colonizers, including the expressive forms they were embodied in—storytelling, music, and dance—they began to develop new, hybrid cultural idioms that mixed these new forms with traditional ones. In time, the tools of the colonizer became the tools of the colonized, as Africans in the Americas learned Western languages and then began to read in its literatures. On the Indian continent, first Mughal writings and then the entire corpus of English literature were absorbed by successive generations of South Asians. The same thing happened across the African continent, from Morocco to South Africa. And, during the twentieth century, colonized people from these countries, and more, began to study abroad at educational institutions in the West. Transnational literature is, in many ways, the stepchild of this complex and ironic history.

Of course, none of this justifies colonialism, and the systematic forms of violence and suppression it unleashed. It does, however, call attention to the paradoxical effects colonialism had on culture in general and literary production in particular. Conquest, colonization, empire, and their undoing over the course of the twentieth century, linked as each of them was to economic and cultural globalization, ultimately reshaped literary production across the globe, not only in formerly colonized regions of the world but in the metropolitan centers of European and American colonialism as well. Of course, colonialism and postcolonialism have had dramatically uneven effects on literary production, circulation, and the evolution of transnational literature. On the one hand, colonialism involved the violent suppression of indigenous culture, art, and storytelling, yet on the other hand it set in motion a complex set of forces that led to the kind of cultural contamination Appiah has argued is central to human interaction generally, whether that interaction be violent or peaceful. Crucially, the forms of exchange here, while uneven, were two-way. Literary texts from the West became increasingly ubiquitous in colonized regions of the world, in many cases introducing there the particularly Western idea of literature as a special and a privileged aesthetic medium, while at the same time marginalizing and attempting to trivialize indigenous writings, whether in the forms of Aztec Codices or Indian epics like the *Mahabharata* or the *Ramayana*. However, at the same time, indigenous literature became of interest first to Western scholars, and then to Western readers and writers. By the nineteenth century a kind of global traffic in literary works from all parts of the world had begun, which is why writers like Goethe began to realize there might be such a thing as *world literature*.

The second thing that happened as a result of colonialism, and in its aftermath, was that the production, and eventually the subject matter, of literature began to change as formerly colonized people began to write literature—in their own languages, but also in English, Spanish, Portuguese, and French, to cite just a few. Early prominent examples would be the Mexican nun, Juana Inés de la Cruz (1648–1695), whose works include a wide range of poetry, drama, and philosophy, and the African writer, Olaudah Equiano (1745–1797), author of *The Interesting Narrative of the Life of Olaudah Equiano, Or Gustavus Vassa, The African* (1789). By the mid-nineteenth century, literature in English by former African slaves like Phyllis Wheatley and Fredrick Douglass was becoming an increasingly important component of what first became African American literature and then literature associated with the African Diaspora. The same thing happened, of course, in Africa itself, and in South Asia and the Caribbean. Education in the languages, histories, and literatures of colonizing nations led inevitably to the production of literary works in English, French, Spanish, and other languages by indigenous writers in each of these regions. And of course, and at the same time, the history and experience of colonization became an increasingly popular subject in both European and American literature. Not only did writers like Herman Melville, Mark Twain, and Rudyard Kipling write about their own experiences abroad, but, as Edward Said has shown in his book on the treatment of colonialism in the nineteenth-century English novel (*Culture and Imperialism*, 1993), the topic became an increasingly central one for the English novel as well.

The production of postcolonial and transnational literatures accelerated dramatically, as we have already noted, in the context of decolonization and independence, especially after the Second World War. Here we need to pause to address the question, what is decolonization? Broadly speaking, decolonization simply refers to the process of undoing the effects of colonization. However, those effects are myriad, and deeply entrenched. Some have to do with concrete, material structures—political, governmental, bureaucratic—while others are related to social, religious, and cultural matters, and with identity itself. Postcolonial critics, for example, have written at length about the colonization of consciousness. Consciousness, briefly put, refers to an individual's awareness of his or her own existence and state of mind, and is characterized by our experiences of thoughts, sensations, and emotions. Consciousness, however, is not simply a biological or cognitive state. It is shaped by culturally specific beliefs, social practices, and political ideologies. We like to think that there is something universal about the "human condition," and at a general level this is certainly true. Driven by our need for food and shelter, procreation, and the desire to protect ourselves from harm, humans have developed similar communal practices and belief systems. However, human diversity reflects how radically different social, cultural, and belief systems have evolved, and those different systems shape human consciousness in culturally specific ways. Human consciousness is not only biological. It is socially constructed, and when a social system is imposed violently on a people from the outside, part of what gets transformed is the very consciousness of those people. For this reason, decolonization unfolds at a very personal level and has to do with the challenge of undoing the colonization of individual identity, a process, we shall see, that is regularly explored in transnational literature.

Of course, decolonization also has to do with complex questions about how to realign social, political, and cultural systems after colonization. For this reason, decolonization can produce spirited debates about how to reconcile modernity and tradition, and can often raise vexing questions. How, for example, do colonized peoples recover their indigenous identities? Is such a recovery even possible? What is to be done about religious and cultural practices suppressed or banned under colonization? Are they deeply connected to the "spirit" or "essence" of people, and do they, for this reason, need to be recuperated? Or do these terms name historical ideas or ideals that always give way to other, newer ones? What about beliefs and practices that conflict with modern life or which are even deemed to undermine economic development? Are they to be rekindled because they are intrinsic to a people's personal, social, cultural, and even political identities, or set aside in the interests of modernization? Again, we will see later that these questions recur in a wide range of transnational fiction, poetry, and drama.

It is worth noting, as well, that when individual nations undergo the process of decolonization, the process is itself a transnational phenomenon. That is, successful struggles for self-determination among a myriad of formerly colonized nations have also had a profound collective effect on the autonomy and agency of people across the globe. These struggles have come in a variety of forms, from peaceful and armed resistance to civil wars and the intervention of international agencies like the UN, or individual foreign countries. Understood as a collective global phenomenon, decolonization has had a profound effect on the transnational flow of people and culture in particular. This may seem ironic, since decolonization has as its main aim the establishment of free and independent nations. However, decolonization has contributed to the strengthening and solidarity of formerly marginalized peoples in ways that have been economically and culturally empowering beyond the confines of the nation-state. It has also contributed to the mobility across increasingly fluid borders of large populations of people, ranging from those who become refugees as a result of the sometimes-violent effects of struggles for independence, and others who, through employment or educational opportunities, are able to transform their lives in the very metropolitan centers that supported colonialism.

Transnational literature both dramatizes the challenges of decolonization in all of its forms, and works itself to effect decolonization. Chimamanda Ngozi Adichie, for example (as we shall see in more detail later), captures the entire historical sweep of colonization and decolonization, albeit in abbreviated form, in her story, "The Headstrong Historian," which concludes *The Thing Around Your Neck* (2009). Jhumpa Lahiri's "When Mr. Pirzada Came to Dine" (in her early collection, *The Interpreter of Maladies*, 1999), written from the point of view a young Pakistani-American girl, explores how her sense of her own identity becomes reshaped as she comes to learn about the complex history of colonialism—and its aftermath, in Pakistan and Bangladesh. Later, we will explore a more extended, multifaceted treatment of decolonization in Zakes Mda's novel, *The Heart of Redness* (2000), which deals with post-apartheid South Africa and the tensions that develop there around competing commitments to tradition and modernity, and the way in which they inform both economic development and individual identity, topics we shall see taken up as well by Namwali Serpell in *The Old Drift*, her 2019 novel set in Zambia.

While, as we have already indicated, there are important links between transnational and postcolonial literature, it is important to distinguish between them. Where "transnational," as we have seen, puts the emphasis on movement across and between two or more entities, "postcolonial," in the most literal sense of the word, refers to a time period, post or after colonization. However, the term is also often used to describe a condition under which people live, or to resistance to that condition. It is also used to categorize forms of writing that are specifically about that condition and its history. In both senses, then, the term postcolonial clearly relates to a range of phenomena that are transnational. For example, the condition of *being* postcolonial exists both among people in formerly colonized regions that have become independent, and among people that have migrated from those colonies to Western countries, and is thus the product of transnational forces. The same can be said with regard to postcolonial literature. It is the product of intersecting transnational forces—military, political, social, and cultural. It would be impossible, then, to explore the nation, subjectivity, culture, or literature from a postcolonial perspective without at the same time studying it from a transnational perspective, and vice versa. This helps, of course, to explain the substantial overlap between the study of postcolonial and transnational literatures.

However, by almost any measure, transnational literature, as a category, is much broader than the one we call postcolonial. While the term "postcolonial" references a set of historically and politically specific forces related to imperialism, colonialism, and resistance movements that led to decolonization and independence, "transnational" is a much broader term used with reference to the movement across national borders characteristic of a range of commercial and cultural formations—films, humanitarian groups, corporations, food, literature, etc. In addition, as both a literary form ("postcolonial literature") and an institutionalized academic practice ("postcolonial studies") the term postcolonial has a much different set of references than transnational. "Transnational studies," to the extent the term is used by scholars to designate a field or specialty, refers in a general way to the global study of political, economic, health, environmental, cultural, and diplomatic subjects with a much wider range than those covered in postcolonial studies.

Notwithstanding these important distinctions, however, it is certainly the case that in practice literary works studied as postcolonial texts are often also studied as examples of transnational literature (the texts cited above are examples). Indeed, many of the texts discussed throughout this book deal in some way with imperialism, colonialism, decolonization, and the postcolonial condition, and for this reason are regularly treated under the auspices of postcolonial literature. One of the risks, however, of simply folding postcolonial literature into the category of transnational literature, in effect, treating it as a subset of a larger category, is that a focus on the specific history and politics of colonialism and postcolonialism can end up becoming obscured. For this reason, it is important in discussing postcolonial literature from the perspective of transnational literature, to foreground the specificity of its relationship to the historical forces of colonization and decolonization, and its specific focus on the postcolonial condition.

BORDER STUDIES

Like postcolonial studies, the field of border studies has since the early 1980s played a significant role in transnationalizing literary studies. The study of borders and border zones first took shape in the 1960s as an interdisciplinary practice combining work in the social and natural sciences in fields as varied as geography, political science, sociology, anthropology, and environmental studies. This work tended to focus on the nature, function, and history of geographic and legal borders, but by the 1980s scholars in literary and cultural studies began to take an increasing interest in the cultural dimensions of borders and border zones. As Alexander C. Diener and Joshua Hagen point out in *Borders: A Very Short Introduction* (2012), borders can be both official and unofficial (12), they can have both "material and symbolic dimensions" (121). Examples of material borders include geographical formations like rivers and mountain ranges, while official borders inscribe into law divisions between everything from private, individually owned property to local, regional, and state borders, as well as borders between nations. Unofficial, or symbolic borders, on the other hand, are socially and historically constructed binary distinctions used to regulate social and cultural norms and behavior. Obvious traditional examples would include categories used to distinguish between races, genders, sexual orientations, and ethnicities, although in each of these cases, of course, the inflexible and even arbitrary nature of these distinctions has become clear, and they have given way to increasingly fluid and flexible ways of thinking about difference that sees such borders as arbitrary.

Attention to the cultural dimensions of borders, and a particular interest in social and cultural production in border zones, had a particular impact on literary studies, especially in the United States, where borders studies in the humanities and social sciences began to take formal, institutional shape around the study of cultural production along the U.S./Mexican border. Fostered by pioneering texts like Gloria Anzaldúa's *Borderlands/La Frontera: The New Mestiza* (1987), and the work of novelists and poets such as Ana Castillo, Sandra Cisneros, Rolando Hinojosa, Pat Mora, and Luis Alberto Urrea, as well as critics and scholars including Ilan Stavans, Ramón Saldvar, and Norma Alarcón, work in this field exerted an increasing influence in the 1980s and 1990s, engendering a proliferation of work on border writing—and the relationship between borders and identity, belonging, and cultural practices—that became increasingly transnational. Given the global ubiquity—and vexed nature—of nation-state borders, and, perhaps more importantly, given the inherently transnational nature of border zones, it is hardly surprising that the work pioneered by border studies focused on the U.S./Mexican border began to influence scholarly and critical study of other border zones in places like the Middle East, South Asia, Europe, and the Americas, such as Israel and Palestine, India and Pakistan, Ireland and England, the nations spread throughout island regions like the Caribbean, the Bay of Bengal, and the Indian Ocean.

This work, collectively, calls attention both to the historical and cultural contingency of borders, and the fact that scholars and critics create the locations that they study. The focus on literary and cultural production in border zones like those mentioned above pays attention, as well, to interactive, hybrid, and deeply syncretic spaces, liminal zones in which cultural exchange is the norm. A focus on border zones serves, as well, to productively dislocate and unsettle a traditional focus on literary and cultural production within the fixed borders of nations, and to call attention to what goes on in the liminal margins between them. At the same time that it puts a focus on the sometimes eccentric nature of the local, it calls attention to the fluid relationship between local and global forces. Mary Louise Pratt, for example, called early attention to what she called "contact zones," spaces characterized by "colonial encounters, the space in which peoples geographically and historically separated come into contact with each other and establish ongoing relations, usually involving conditions of coercion, radical inequality, and intractable conflict" (*Imperial Eyes: Travel Writing and Transculturation*, 1992, 4). Similarly, the Caribbean writer and critic, Édouard Glissant, in an essay on the novel in the Americas, argued that its most prominent borders when it came to literary production were not national but cultural. From his perspective, novelists of the American northeast, like Henry James and Ernest Hemingway, and those of the south, like William Faulkner, belonged to two distinguishable *cultural zones* (*Caribbean Discourse*, 1989). In his view, the historical context of Faulkner's interest in race and cultural difference marked his connection with an essentially Caribbean cultural matrix, while James and Hemingway were working in a cultural zone dominated by Europe. Each zone, in his view, has had a different relationship to modernity, and so, while all three are "American" writers, Faulkner, unlike James and Hemingway, is connected to a cultural and literary framework with roots in the American south, and, through places like New Orleans, to the Caribbean (this is particularly the case with his novel, *Absalom, Absalom!*, 1936).

Formulations like these helped contribute to the focus on regional rather than national borders for the organization of literary and cultural study. Rob Wilson, for example, in *Reimagining the American Pacific* (2000), stresses how geographical spaces are turned into regions by the scholars who study them, a process he conceived of as "regionalizing spaces" (236). Regions like the "Asia Pacific," or what Paul Gilroy called "the Black Atlantic," are shaped into a kind of "coherence and consensus" (235) around a focus on "cross-border flows of information, labor, finance, media images, and global commodities" in a zone that transcends nation-state boundaries (233). Wilson is as interested in studying *how* areas become regionalized by scholars, a focus he calls "critical regionalism" (248), as much as he is interested in studying the regions themselves, because his primary interest is in calling attention to the creation of regions or borders as something scholars and critics perform.

Broadly speaking, border studies in each of the iterations discussed above has served to focus attention on intersectional, marginal, and liminal spaces of interest to transnational writers and the scholars who study them. Together, they reflect what the critic Walter Mignolo calls "border thinking" ("The Many Faces of Cosmo-polis: Border Thinking and Critical Cosmopolitanism," 2000, 736), thinking that takes place *across* rather than *between* borders and that focuses on "silenced and marginalized voices" (736).

GLOBALIZATION STUDIES

In recent decades, the study of globalization has exploded across the social sciences and the humanities in general, and has also had a dramatic effect on the comparative study of literatures in each of the forms discussed above. Globalization studies has helped shift the ground upon which comparative literature, and postcolonial and border studies were built, and has helped in significant ways to shape both transnational literature and its study. Indeed, the forces of economic and cultural globalization have been so central to the creation, circulation, and study of transnational literature that it is tempting think of them as the same thing, to understand the category "transnational literature" as signaling the globalization of literature. It now nearly goes without saying that "literature" is a collective product of the forces of economic and cultural globalization that had been accelerating since at least the sixteenth century, and which facilitated the increasing mobility of literary works fueled by a range of printing and shipping technologies. Understood as an economic commodity, books have become thoroughly incorporated into a business model defined by globalization. The production and circulation of Western literature is now an international business in which books are translated and marketed for a global audience. Perhaps more importantly, with the increasing popularity of literature from formerly ignored or marginalized countries in Asia, South Asia, Africa, and the Caribbean, the ubiquity and rapidity of translation has now insured that their circulation will be global. If we add to this the fact that much contemporary fiction, poetry, drama, and creative non-fiction is written in English by writers from countries as disparate as Nigeria, Trinidad-Tobago, Bosnia, India, Pakistan, and China, the phrase "transnational literature" almost seems redundant. And, of course, the Internet insures that texts by contemporary writers, interviews with and articles about them, and their social media feeds, will be available everywhere and always.

Another link between transnational literature and globalization, of course, is the fact that an increasing range of literary works published in the last four decades are *about* globalization. Many of them focus on the transnational effects of its economic, cultural, demographic, and psychological dimensions. Indeed, most of the literary works discussed in Part II of this book engage the forces of globalization in both explicit and implicit ways, whether through a focus on its economic dimension (examples include Mohsin Hamid's *How to Get Filthy Rich in Rising Asia*, 2013, Zia Haider Rahman's *In the Light of What We Know*, 2014, and Zakes Mda's *The Heart of Redness*, 2000), its cultural ramifications (examples here include Chimamanda Ngozi Adichie's collection of stories, *The Thing Around Your Neck*, 2009, Namwali Serpell's *The Old Drift: A Novel*, 2019, and Luis Alberto Urrea's *The House of Broken Angels*, 2018, to name just a few), migration and displacement (Aleksandar Hemon's *The Lazarus Project*, 2008, Helon Habila's *Travelers*, 2019, Hamid's *Exit West*, 2017, Jenny Erpenbeck's *Go, Went, Gone*, 2017), or its political upheavals (Viet Thanh Nguyen's *The Sympathizer*, 2015, Jhumpa Lahiri's *The Lowland*, 2013, and Derek Walcott's *Omeros*, 1990). The extent to which these forces intersect to form a network of overlapping effects is exemplified by the fact that most of the literary works mentioned above, by writers from countries as disparate as Pakistan, South Africa, Nigeria, Zambia, Mexico, Bosnia, and Germany, deal simultaneously with the economic, cultural, demographic, and psychological effects of globalization.

While the terms "global" and "transnational" are often used interchangeably, there are some key differences between them. The term global, which predates transnational by a few decades, refers to any entity or phenomenon that can be thought of as involving the entire world (whether related to communication, travel, corporations, or cultural commodities from music to food). In contrast, transnational, as we have already noted, has a more general meaning suggesting fluidity or mobility, with its emphasis on moving across, beyond, or transcending geographic, cultural, or national borders. Moreover, while the term transnational is regularly used as a general modifying term for something global in scope, *globalization* refers more specifically to the acceleration of economic, communication, technological, and cultural systems that have made national borders increasingly redundant, although it is important to note that many critics follow Roland Robertson in seeing globalization as a long historical phenomenon dating back at least to the fifteenth century (see *Globalization: Social Theory and Global Culture*, 1992). While globalization is transnational in scope, the term also has a specifically political dimension that distinguishes it from the more casual meaning of transnational. For example, advocates of economic globalization present it as having a positive economic effect, lifting markets and contributing to rising incomes almost everywhere, while critics call attention to its uneven and negative effects (the tension between these two assessments is reflected in many of the literary works cited above). Some critics who write about cultural globalization, as we have already noted, insist that it has liberating effects, while others are deeply troubled by its tendency to produce cultural homogenization (another topic that runs through much transnational literature). So, while the two terms certainly overlap, their differences are important to keep in mind. While globalization has transnational effects, the term has some very different connotations. Likewise, speaking out in favor of transnationalism is not always the same thing as endorsing globalization.

One of the criticisms of globalization is that it is a vehicle for Westernization—the Westernization of economies, political systems, religion, and cultural products and practices. As such, it is often seen as a contemporary version of colonialism. And yet, it can be misleading to see contemporary globalization as a purely Western phenomenon, since countries like Japan and China have contributed greatly to economic globalization, and the circulation of cultural forms and practices—including literature—has no single source but rather is formed by complex patterns of circulation, absorption, transformation, and recirculation. Moreover, if we follow critics like Robertson and see globalization as a set of forces that accelerated dramatically in the twentieth century but have a long history, the intersectional nature of globalization becomes even clearer. Janet Abu-Lughod, for example, pointed out long ago that economic systems connecting Europe with China and the Middle East had already developed by the fourteenth century, and that many of the commodities and technologies traded during this period came from the East to the West (*Before European Hegemony: The World System A.D. 1250–1350*, 1989). Likewise, the Nobel Prize winning economist, Amartya Sen, has insisted that the world has been undergoing globalization since at least 1000 BC, long before the rise of the West. He calls attention to a "chain of intellectual relations that link Western mathematics and science to a collection of distinctly non-Western practitioners," insisting that "the agents of globalization are neither European nor exclusively Western, nor are they necessarily linked to Western dominance" ("How to Judge Globalism," 2002).

If transnational literature, then, is a product of globalization, it is not simply the product of a flow from West to East in which the dominant forces are Western, but rather, the product of a complex set of interconnected streams that flow back-and-forth through endless circuits characterized by appropriation and transformation. While it is certainly the case that globalization involves the spread of Western foods, music, film, and literature across the globe in ways that can seem to marginalize or undermine traditional cultural practices, it is also the case that foods, music, film, and literature increasingly flow *toward* the West from the east and Global South, deeply influencing cultural practices there as well. What these intersecting streams produce are hybrid or syncretic cultural forms and practices born from systems of production, circulation, absorption, adaptation, and recirculation. As Kwame Anthony Appiah has argued, cultural authenticity is, more often than not, the product of "cosmopolitan contamination" (*Cosmopolitanism: Ethics in a World of Strangers*, 101), the intersection and melding of different cultural practices, so that "trying to find some primordially authentic culture can be like peeling an onion" (107). And, like Abu-Lughod and Sen, Appiah points out such contamination has a very long history:

> [T]he migrations that have contaminated the larger world were not all modern. Alexander's empire molded both the states and the sculpture of Egypt and North India; first the Mongols then the Mughals shaped great swaths of Asia; the Bantu migrations populated half the African continent. Islamic states stretch from Morocco to Indonesia ... The traders of the Silk Road changed the style of elite dress in Italy; someone brought Chinese pottery for burial in fifteenth-century Swahili graves.
>
> (112)

DIASPORA STUDIES

The historical, cultural, and geographic study of diaspora and diaspora communities has also contributed to the transnationalization of literary studies. Diaspora communities have an ancient history, but they have proliferated dramatically as a result of contemporary geopolitical forces, including decolonization, hyper-nationalism, ethnic cleansing, civil strife, and, of course, the uneven and often disruptive effects of globalization. The term *diaspora* is derived from the Greek word *diaspeirein*, which means to scatter about or disperse. This, in turn, is derived from *dia*, meaning about or across, which of course links the term to the prefix *trans* in *transnational*. The word first became associated with the Jewish diaspora, produced by the ancient dispersion of Jews from the Holy Land, and fueled much later by the holocaust. Often linked to the term *exile*, diaspora has since come to be used to refer to any demographic group existing in significant numbers in communities outside of its homeland, hence terms like African diaspora and South Asian diaspora, both of which were produced by the slave trade and indentured servitude. Diaspora communities can be the product of overt discrimination and the exercise of brute power—enslavement, religious or ethnic cleansing, expulsion, civil war, etc.—but are also fueled by economic inequality and the absence of educational opportunities.

Studying the forces that have produced, and continue to produce, global diasporas, is, like border studies, a broadly interdisciplinary enterprise involving both the social sciences and the humanities. This work, collectively, explores the political, social, and cultural forces that have shaped the forced migration or displacement experienced by diasporic communities. It is particularly interested in diasporic subjectivity, that is, in how identity is shaped by the experience of displacement, dispersion, and resettling among diasporic peoples, especially with regard to how they negotiate the relationship between the culture of their homeland and that of the nation or region in which they have settled (keeping in mind that something like African or South Asian diasporic subjectivity is going to be shaped both by a shared relationship to homeland and the different cultural forces and values at work in the disparate places where African or South Asian peoples reside). The connection to a homeland, of course, can be concrete and political, characterized by forms of activism and intervention, but also subjective, characterized by emotional, psychological, and cultural forms of connection.

Because the experience of diasporic peoples involves cross-border migrations that are often deeply connected to complex histories of colonization, and to the contemporary effects of both decolonization and globalization, the study of diaspora per se, and diasporic literature in particular, intersects with border, postcolonial, and globalization studies. For this reason, as we have already noted, scholarly interest deeply intersects with, and is in fact largely driven by, the work of transnational writers whose own experiences have been shaped by displacement, and a deep-felt connection to diasporic communities. This work, as we shall see in more detail throughout Part II of this book, is broadly engaged with exploring histories of displacement and forced migration, with the experience of personal and cultural estrangement, and with the pull of homeland as it comes into conflict with the pressures involved in settling into, making a living in, and adjusting to a new, and often culturally strange place. In this literature, memory and longing tied to the past shape identity and experience in a present dominated by a whole range of new forces. Deep roots in a homeland organized around tradition exist simultaneously with the growth of what becomes, inevitably, an increasingly hybrid and syncretic subjectivity. This is a key subject, for example, in Zadie Smith's *White Teeth* (2001), a novel about two intersecting diasporas in contemporary London, South Asian and Caribbean, in a story that centers on multiple conflicts between purity and hybridity. The burgeoning Caribbean diaspora in Great Britain is also the subject of the Jamaican poet, Louise Bennett's poem, "Colonization in Reverse." Cristina Garcia's novel, *Dreaming in Cuban* (1992), moves back-and-forth between Cuba as homeland, and diasporic Cuban communities in New York City and Florida. As its title suggest, the book deals both with diasporic dreams about the homeland (in its personal, political, and cultural dimensions), and dreams of making a new life in America. Later, Junot Díaz's novel, *The Brief Wondrous Life of Oscar Wao* (2007), explored in its own original way the same terrain with respect to the Dominican Republic and New Jersey. Nearly all of the novels and stories by Jhumpa Lahiri and Chimamanda Ngozi Adichie move their readers in a perpetual back-and-forth between contemporary homelands in South Asia and Africa, and contemporary diasporic communities in North America. Teju Cole's *Open City* (2011) features a narrator from Nigeria living in New York City whose relationship to the African diaspora there is vexed and troubled. While in Brussels, Belgium, he falls in with a small community of North African refugees whose plight intersects with those of the characters the narrator has met in New York. These are among just a few of the literary works dealing with the diasporic condition we will have occasion to discuss in Part II.

Taken together, these approaches to studying literature in a transnational context represent a collective attempt, which accelerated dramatically in the decades after the Second World War, to broaden the scope and nature of literary inquiry in a way that responded to the proliferation of literary writing from around the globe. While each one represents a distinct field of specialization, the approaches overlap with and influence each other in a variety of ways. The acceleration of transnational writing in the last half of the twentieth century is matched by the steady development of approaches to its study, so that transnational literary studies is best understood as a kind of palimpsest, a succession of writing about literature in a transnational context from positons that have been layered over one another so as to become, to a degree, indistinguishable. While the fields of world literature, comparative literature, postcolonial literature, border literature, and diaspora literature constitute separate and coherent fields of study, the differences of which certainly need to be recognized, transnational literary studies draw on each of them in ways that inevitably link them. As we shall see in Part II, when we turn to the literature itself, transnational fiction, poetry, and drama engage issues that cut across the concerns of each of these fields, so that the strategies of reading and analysis they have each developed all become crucial to its understanding.

FURTHER READING

Ashcroft, Bill. *Post-Colonial Studies: The Key Concepts* (New York: Routledge, 2013).

Diener, Alexander C. and Joshua Hagan. *Borders: A Very Short Introduction* (Oxford: Oxford University Press, 2012).

Hutchinson, Ben. *Comparative Literature: A Very Short Introduction* (Oxford: Oxford University Press, 2018).

Jay, Paul. *Global Matters: The Transnational Turn in Literary Studies* (Ithaca: Cornell University Press, 2010).

Lazarus, Neil. *The Cambridge Companion to Postcolonial Literary Studies* (Cambridge: Cambridge University Press, 2004).

Saussy, Haun. *Comparative Literature in an Age of Globalization* (Baltimore: Johns Hopkins University Press, 2006).

Wilson, Janet, and Klaus Stierstorfer, eds. *The Routledge Diaspora Studies Reader* (New York: Routledge, 2018).

REFERENCES

Abu-Lughod, Janet. *Before European Hegemony: The World System A.D. 1250–1350* (Oxford: Oxford University Press, 1989).

Adichie, Chimamanda Ngozi. *The Thing Around Your Neck* (New York: Random House, 2009).

Anzaldúa, Gloria. *Borderlands/La Frontera: The New Mestiza* (San Francisco: Aunt Lute Books, 1987).

Appiah, Kwame Anthony, *Cosmopolitanism: Ethics in a World of Strangers* (New York: W.W. Norton, 2006).

Chakrabarry, Dipesh. *Provincializing Europe: Postcolonial Thought and Historical Difference* (Princeton: Princeton University Press, 2000).

Cole, Teju. *Open City* (New York: Random House, 2011).

Díaz, Junot. *The Brief Wondrous Life of Oscar Wao* (New York: Riverhead, 2007).

Diener, Alexander C. and Joshua Hagen. *Borders: A Very Short Introduction* (Oxford: Oxford University Press, 2012).

Equiano, Olaudah. *The Interesting Narrative and Other Writings* (New York: Penguin, 1995 [1789]).

Erpenbeck, Jenny. *Go, Went, Gone* (New York: New Directions, 2017).

Faulkner, William. *Absalom, Absalom!* (New York: Random House, 1936).

Garcia, Cristina. *Dreaming in Cuban* (New York: Knopf, 1992).

Glissant, Édouard. *Caribbean Discourse* (Charlottesville: University Press of Virginia, 1989).

Habila, Helon. *Travelers* (New York: W.W. Norton, 2019).

Hamid, Mohsin. *How to Get Filthy Rich in Rising Asia* (New York: Riverhead, 2013).

Hamid, Mohsin. *Exit West* (New York: Riverhead, 2017).

Hemon, Aleksandar. *The Lazarus Project* (New York: Riverhead, 2008).

Lahiri, Jhumpa. *Interpreter of Maladies* (Boston: Houghton Mifflin, 1999).

Lahiri, Jhumpa. *The Lowland* (New York: Vintage, 2013).

Mda, Zakes. *The Heart of Redness* (New York: Farrar, Straus and Giroux, 2000).

Mignolo, Walter. "The Many Faces of Cosmo-polis: Border Thinking and Critical Cosmopolitanism," in *Public Culture*, 12 (3), 2000, 736.

Nguyen, Viet Thanh. *The Sympathizer* (New York: Grove Press, 2015).

Pratt, Mary Louise. *Imperial Eyes: Travel Writing and Transculturation* (New York: Routledge, 1992).

Rahman, Zia Haider. *In the Light of What We Know* (New York: Farrar, Straus and Giroux, 2014).

Robertson, Roland. *Globalization: Social Theory and Global Culture* (London: Sage, 1992).

Said, Edward. *Culture and Imperialism* (New York: Knopf, 1993).

Sen, Amartya. "How to Judge Globalism." Retrieved at https://prospect.org/features/judge-globalism.

Serpell, Namwali. *The Old Drift: A Novel* (New York: Random House, 2019).

Smith, Zadie. *White Teeth* (New York: Vintage, 2001)

Urrea, Luis Alberto. *The House of Broken Angels* (New York: Little, Brown and Company, 2018).

Walcott, Derek. *Omeros* (New York: Farrar, Straus and Giroux, 1990).

Wilson, Rob. *Reimagining the American Pacific: From South Pacific to Bamboo Ridge and Beyond* (Durham: Duke University Press, 2000).

Ziolkowski, Jan M. "Incomparable: The Destiny of Comparative Literature, Globalization or Not," in *The Global South*, 1 (2), 2007, 16–44.

WHAT IS TRANSNATIONAL LITERATURE?

Since, as we have already seen, "trans" always implies mobility or movement across or between places, and "national" refers both to cultural communities and to legally constituted nation-states, it would seem that transnational literature is simply literature that, through its production, circulation, and reception, moves across national boundaries. However, since nearly all literature has the capacity for such mobility, this does not get us very far, especially if we are interested in conceiving of transnational literature as a coherent, clearly definable kind of literature. Literary works as wide-ranging as *The Epic of Gilgamesh, The Mahabharata, One Thousand and One Nights, Dante's Divine Comedy*, the plays of Shakespeare, Goethe's *Faust*, the novels of Jane Austen and Emily Bronte, Mark Twain's *Huckleberry Finn*, and *The Narrative of the Life of Frederick Douglas* have all circulated widely on a global scale. However, there is little that links them together as a kind of literature, a body of works that share an identifiable set of subjects, and employ literary forms and devices suited to their exploration. Nor is there any historical context for this way of thinking about transnational literature. That is, while categories like Romantic, Modern, and Postcolonial literature get their coherence in part from the fact that the literature they reference emerged out of and responded specifically to a set of historical, social, cultural, and political developments, transnational literature conceived simply as literature which has circulated widely beyond national boundaries has no such coherence. Lacking any historical context, and without a shared set of subjects, forms, or literary devices, transnational literature seems like an impossibly broad and unwieldy category.

WORLD LITERATURE

As we noted earlier, the challenges involved in conceptualizing transnational literature in this kind of way are dramatized by the relatively new scholarly field called "world literature." Like transnational literature, the phrase "world literature" refers both to an academic field of study and a body of literature, and it puts an emphasis on studying the economic and cultural modes of production, circulation, and reception that make literature a transnational phenomenon. While the idea of world literature began to achieve prominence in the mid-1990s, the concept has its roots in the early nineteenth-century concept of *Weltliteratur*, formulated by the German writer, Johann Wolfgang von Goethe (1749–1832). Goethe, writing in 1801, "hoped that people will soon be convinced that there is no such thing as patriotic art or patriotic science." Rather, he insisted, both "belong, like all good things, to the whole world, and can be fostered only by untrammeled intercourse among all contemporaries, continually bearing in mind what we have inherited from the past" (quoted in Fritz Strich, *Goethe and World Literature*, 1949, 35). By 1827, Goethe had become "convinced a universal world literature is in the process of being constituted" (Goethe, *Essays on Art and Literature*, ed. John Gearey, Goethe's Collected Works, 1986, 225).

What happened to this early nineteenth-century vision of literature as something produced by "the whole world," as art that can be "fostered" by "intercourse among all contemporaries" regardless of national affiliation, to the idea that art is not a form of "patriotic" expression but of "universal" expression? Briefly put, it was side-tracked by the solidification and increasing power of the nation-state in the decades immediately after Goethe's vision of *Weltliteratur*, marginalized by Western colonialism, and justified by the imperialist fantasy that literature is a specifically Western achievement, a product of European races that marked the greatness of Western civilization, a conception that often worked hand-in-glove with the military, economic, educational and judicial institutions of colonialism to suppress and expunge the linguistic, narrative, and expressive practices of colonized people. Over the course of the nineteenth century, literature in both Europe and the United States came to be thought of as the embodiment of the nation, and an expressive form of its nature.

In the United States, writers like Emerson and Whitman insisted that America would never be a great nation until it produced a great literature, and in England Matthew Arnold was instrumental in making sure that an education in literature would be used to shape the citizenship of a rising working class. At the same time, British colonial rule in India was based in part on the suppression of indigenous literary works and the teaching of British history, fiction, poetry, and drama.

For all of these reasons, Goethe's ideal of *Weltliteratur*—whether thought of as a way to conceptualize literature generally, or as an organizing principle for the study of literature—increasingly took a back seat to the familiar nation-state model. Characterized by a focus on the interconnection between literature, identity, culture, and the nation, this model shaped the writing of literary history, and helped to define the curriculum for a literary education in Europe, the United States, and many other countries. It became second nature to divide programs and academic departments according to modern nation-state borders, with Goethe's vision of world literature cordoned off into the separate field of comparative literature. Well into the middle of the twentieth century, a literary education was organized into separate national units such as French, Spanish, Italian, English, or American literature.

For all of these reasons, Goethe's conception of literature as a transnational enterprise received little attention until the waning of colonialism, the rise of postcolonial nations, and the accelerating forces of globalization converged to reassert the transnational nature of literary production and to underscore the importance of non-Western literature. With this convergence, critics have increasingly come to treat the history of literature as a transnational affair, courses and curricula in higher education have become transnational both in terms of the writers and the subject matter they teach, and the structure of the programs they offer (under such categories as multicultural, postcolonial, global, in addition to world literature). Perhaps more significantly, the contemporary production of literature has itself become transnational, whether measured by the range of its authors and the circulation of its texts, or in terms of the substantive issues it engages (globalization, migration, displacement, exile, accelerating cultural hybridity, the proliferation of diasporic communities and identities, etc.).

As a key example of these developments, the field of world literature has proved to be valuable in a number of ways. First of all, it has called attention to how the whole idea of literature became appropriated by the nation state during the nineteenth century in a way that came to obscure our understanding of literature as a fundamentally transnational phenomenon. "As a result of the appropriation of literatures and literary histories by political nations during the nineteenth century," notes Pascale Casanova, "our literary unconscious is largely national."

> Our instruments of analysis and evaluation are national. Indeed the study of literature almost everywhere in the world is organized along national lines. This is why we are blind to a certain number of trans-national phenomena that have permitted a specifically literary world to gradually emerge over the past four centuries or so.
>
> (*The World Republic of Letters*, 2007, xi)

The resurgence of the concept of world literature exemplifies how literary studies in recent decades has undergone a transnational turn, not so much a reorientation away from the study of literature in the context of the nation, but a complicating of that orientation that focuses on the transnational dimensions of literature in general, and the global scope of literary production in regions of the world (Africa, the Caribbean, South Asia, the Global South, etc.) formerly marginalized by a focus on Western literature.

Another key contribution world literature studies has made rests in its focus on the historical modes of production, circulation, and reception that have always shaped literary culture globally. Given the prominence of close reading, and the orientation of literary studies around the analysis and interpretation of the meaning of individual works, relatively little attention had been paid throughout much of the twentieth century to literary works as commodities, to understanding the role of economic systems, technology, modes of circulation, and the politics of reception in shaping that culture. This is not only a central facet of world literature studies, but in fact, it constitutes its core definition. According to the prominent world literature scholar David Damrosch, the term "world literature" does not in fact refer to a kind of literature but to an approach to literary study. World literature, Damrosch, insists, is not "a canon of works but rather a mode of circulation and of reading" (*What is World Literature?*, 5).

The problem here, of course, is that if the term "world literature" does not refer to a kind of literature but rather to modes of circulation and reading, it would seem there is actually no such thing as world literature. Nevertheless, as Damrosch goes on to point out, world literature scholars have in fact attempted to distinguish between what are, in effect, canons of world literature. They have done so by distinguishing between three approaches to, or categories of, world literature. The first approach has involved conceptualizing world literature as a set of "classic" works of "transcendent, even foundational value," identified in particular with Greek and Roman literature. A second, later one has sought to characterize world literature as a set of "masterpieces" that can be either ancient or modern "and need not have had any foundational cultural force," while a third, more contemporary one sought to conceive of world literature in a less hierarchical or canonical way as a set of "works that would serve as windows into foreign worlds, whether or not these works could be construed as masterpieces" (15). Damrosch does not see these categories as "mutually exclusive" (15), however. Instead he insists "there is really no good reason why we shouldn't allow all three categories their ongoing value" (15).

As helpful as these distinctions may be, they create a number of problems. First of all, the distinction between classics, masterpieces, and foreign literatures retains the kind of hierarchical (and therefore unavoidably elitist) structure contemporary literary culture has sought to move beyond. Terms like "transcendent" and "foundational," historically used to characterize the ostensibly universal value of classical literature and more modern canonical works, have been largely discredited because they instantiate as universal a set of Western, largely Eurocentric values. Indeed, the very concepts of a "classic" or a "masterpiece" are arguably the product of a specifically Western literary discourse and do not necessarily embody categories that have a kind of universal applicability. And "foreign" has to be understood not as an empirical but a relative term, associated in the West all too often with the strange, exotic, and uncivilized. Of course, scholars in world literature have been well aware of these problems, and the field has evolved in response to them. Damrosch points out, for example that, in recent decades, scholars in the field of comparative literature have paid increasing attention to "marginal," "subaltern," and "multicultural literatures" in a context deeply influenced by postcolonial and globalization studies (16), although he cautions that this "modernizing tendency" should not "entail the sheer overwhelming of the past by the present" (17). The danger he worries about here is that "students of imperialism, colonialism, nationalism, and globalization" will "define their topics in such a way as to restrict their investigations to just the last five hundred years of human history, or the last hundred years, or even the last few years" (17). This is a trend that, in his view, can "deprive us of the ability to learn from a much wider range of empires, colonies, polities, and migrations" (17).

Nevertheless, critics such as Emily Apter, writing in *Against World Literature: On the Politics of Untranslatability* (2014), worry that the field of world literature is organized to a fault around a "conservationist attitude," positioning the critic as a kind of "curator" who appraises each literary work's worth (327). Worse still, the "structure of legitimation" is Western and largely organized around aesthetic appreciation. "World Literature," from her point of view, becomes a kind of "global heritage property" (327).

> Severed from place, thrown into the maw of the global culture industry or survey course, and subject to pedagogical transmission by instructors with low levels of cultural literacy and nonexistent knowledge of a translated work's original language, local or native literature relinquishes its defining self-properties once it is exported and trafficked like an artifact.
>
> (326)

Apter's overarching concern, flagged by the subtitle of her book, is that the field of world literature is too dependent on translating the untranslatable. Of course, she has in mind the literal challenge of translating one language into another, the fact that a work deemed to be "world literature" has to be read by a majority of readers in translation (or else by only a select group of scholars in their original language). However, she is also deeply concerned with the "untranslatability" of culture itself, worrying that the ideal of "detached engagement" on the part of the reader Damrosch values (326) is not part of the solution, but part of the problem.

Reading world literature with an eye toward understanding its treatment of something we think of as the universal human condition runs the risk of marginalizing historical and cultural differences that ought to be at the very center of a reader's attention, missing—or mistranslating—the local, the particular, the specific in the humanist act of empathizing with the Other. In Apter's view, a world literature framework runs the risk of promoting "identifying" over "differing" (335).

TRANSNATIONAL LITERATURE

World literature, as we have seen, represents a breathtakingly large historical category running from the classics of Hindu, Islamic, Greek, and Roman cultures all the way up to present-day multi-cultural and postcolonial literatures. In contrast, transnational litera-ture is a particular type of literature, emergent at an identifiable historical moment and dealing, collectively, with a set of issues and themes associated with decolonization, globalization, postmodernity, and technology. Put another way, transnational literature is about the variety of forms of transnational experience produced by the convergence of these forces. Of course, approaches to transnational literature run some of the risks Apter worries about. However, one of the things that distinguishes both transnational literature and its study from the field of world literature is the fact that, collectively, it confronts these concerns head on. In addition to focusing attention on circulation, reception, influence, and intertextuality, transnational literature—and its study—is careful to explore issues surrounding literal and cultural translation, cultural authenticity and appropria-tion, the problem of reducing complex and multifaceted human behaviors to a (largely Eurocentric) universal human condition, and the dangers of flattening out rather than making central the ways in which history shapes human experience.

Whereas world literature starts with the classics and works its way out to the periphery of "foreign worlds," transnational litera-ture takes literature from the periphery as its point of departure. Moreover, it subjects the center/periphery binary to scrupulous theoretical and historical critique. As we will see in more detail a bit later, transnational literature viewed from this perspective is transnational in two specific ways. First, it has its origins in a wide range of regions including Africa, the Caribbean, Asia, and the global South that were ignored or marginalized by the largely Eurocentric and Amerocentric nation-state model of literary studies that evolved in the nineteenth and twentieth centuries. Second, it is associated with authors who have themselves experienced the kind of displacement and mobility characteristic of twentieth- and twenty-first-century life under decolonization, globalization, and the proliferation of struggles related to nationalism around the globe. Transnational literature understood in this way therefore has a kind of thematic coherence lacking in the multitude of texts treated as world literature. Engaged as it is with exploring the social, political, cultural, economic, and social forces associated with imperialism, colonialism, decolonization, and globalization, transnational literature engages a broad range of issues and subjects (migration, displacement, exile, the fluidity of borders both literal and figural, cultural hybridity, identity and citizenship, the status of refugees etc.), which have become pressing in our own time. Simply put, the geographical scope of both the locations this literature treats, and the writers who have produced it, represents a dramatic expansion of literature conceived, produced, circulated, and studied largely within a Eurocentric and American framework.

Like world literature, the term transnational literature has been regularly used to refer both to a kind of literature and a field of study. However, this slippage calls attention to the reciprocal relationship between the two. The more scholars in literary studies in recent years have sought to expand the scope of their work beyond canonical works of European and American literature, striving to find new paradigms for studying literature from formerly ignored minorities and regions (reflected in the rise of multicultural, border, postcolonial, feminist, Latinx, African American, and island studies, among others), the more transnational literary studies have become. At the same time, the more transnational literary studies has become, the more prominent transnational literature itself has become—both inside and outside the academy. Along with this popularity has come a deep interest in the underlying social, cultural, artistic, economic, and political forces that have shaped its subjects. As we shall see in more detail throughout this book, the study of transnational literature has focused not just on the close reading and analysis of individual works, but on an expansive study of how the whole history of colonization and decolonization, economic and cultural globalization in general, and the development of electronic means for the rapid circulation of literary works (and the range of social platforms that mediate that circulation and reception) have made literature in our own time a transnational phenomenon.

In sum, despite the fact that transnational literature refers both to a field of study *and* to a body of literature, we need to distinguish between world literature and transnational literature as bodies of literature. While the field of world literature studies is one of many that both reflect, and contribute to, the transnationalizing of literary studies, transnational literature as a body of writing concerned with transnational experience, defined broadly in the way we have been discussing it, constitutes a much more distinct and historically embedded category of literature than the much larger and more amorphous body of texts treated as world literature.

TRANSNATIONAL WRITERS

Transnational literature, as this book has been stressing, turns our attention to literary production in liminal spaces and border zones, to characters and stories marked by mobility, to texts that explore the experience of migrancy and the formation of new, hybrid identities. This is literature produced, as we have already noted, by what the critic Ariana Dagnino has referred to as "a new generation of culturally mobile writers" who "by choice or by life circumstances, experience cultural dislocation, live transnational experiences, cultivate bilingual-pluri-lingual proficiency, physically immerse themselves in multiple cultures/geographies/territories, expose themselves to diversity and nurture plural, flexible identities" ("Transcultural Writers and Transcultural Literature in the Age of Global Modernity," 2012). Dagnino's focus on the literal and cultural mobility of post-Second World War writers is clearly in synch with Lionnet and Shih's concept of "minor transnationalisms" because it supplements the attention paid to canonical writers whose influence has been global with the reading of literature by formerly ignored or marginalized authors who are particularly interested in writing about displacement, cultural conflict, diasporic experience, and the decidedly contemporary challenges of living across or between national identities.

In his book, *The Great Derangement: Climate Change and the Unthinkable* (2016), the Calcutta-born novelist Amitav Ghosh concisely sketches out how contemporary transnational writing, which he argues began to achieve significant visibility in the 1980s, emerged in the convergence of the political and cultural forces we have been discussing in a way that fostered the emergence of transnational writers like himself. The early 1980s, he writes,

> were a time in which the paradoxical coupling of the processes of decolonization, on the one hand, and the increasing hegemony of the English language, on the other, made it possible for writers like myself to enter the global literary mainstream in a way that had not been possible in the preceding two centuries. At the same time, changes in technologies of communication, and the rapid growth in networks of translation, served to internationalize both politics and literature to a point where it could be said that Goethe's vision of a "world literature" (*Weltliteratur*) had come close to being realized.
>
> (122–3)

While Ghosh's dating of the rise of the transnational writer needs to be pushed back a bit, his sketch of the conditions that made it possible is spot on: the empowerment of formerly marginalized writers that came with decolonization, the ironic fact that many of them came of age as writers working in English, a language they learned in countries as diverse as India and Nigeria under colonial rule, the increasing internationalization of the political world after the Second World War, and the striking development of new technologies of communication which, coupled with the ubiquity of translation, led to the globalization of literary works as both a discursive currency and a cultural commodity. The key point here is that transnational literature is the product of successive generations of highly mobile writers like Ghosh. They include well-known writers who have had a profound influence on younger transnational writers, including among others Wole Soyinka from Nigeria, Ngũgĩ wa Thiong'o from Kenya, Toni Morrison from the United States, Orhan Pamuk from Turkey, Doris Lessing from Zimbabwe and Britain, W.G. Sebald from Germany, Roberto Bolano from Chile, and Elena Ferrante from Italy.

Among the younger writers influenced by their work, consider, for example, the following, who are among those to be discussed in more detail in Part II of this book. Jhumpa Lahiri, author of *The Interpreter of Maladies* and a number of novels, was born in London of Indian parents, but raised in the United States, the country in which she established her reputation as the author of short stories and novels about characters whose lives have been lived in the overlapping spaces between these countries. After achieving prominence, she moved to Rome where she has been writing in Italian and then translating her work back into English. Aleksandar Hemon, author of *The Lazarus Project*, was born in Sarajevo but found himself stranded in Chicago when the Bosnian Civil War broke out in 1992. He taught himself English, studied literature at Northwestern University and Loyola University Chicago, went on to publish a series of acclaimed works in English, won a MacArthur Foundation "genius" award, and continues to write, publish, and speak in both English and Bosnian. Mohsin Hamid, author of *Exit West*, was born in Lahore, Pakistan, moved to California as a child while his father studied at Stanford University, moved back to Pakistan with his family to attend Lahore University, studied creative writing at Princeton University, where he drafted his first novel, *Moth Smoke*, took a law degree from Harvard, worked in New York City as a management consultant for McKinsey and Company, relocated to London, and then moved back to Lahore. He currently splits his time between Lahore, New York, London, and various locations in the Mediterranean. Petina Gappah, international lawyer and author of *Out of Darkness, Shining Light* (2019), was born in Zambia, raised in Zimbabwe, educated in England and Austria, and lived in Geneva, where she worked for the WTO before returning to Harare, Zimbabwe. She has also lived in Berlin. *While Out of Darkness, Shining Light* was written in English, Gappah also writes in her native language, Shona. And, finally, Xiaolu Guo, author of *Nine Continents: A Memoir In And Out of China* (2017), was born in a remote fishing village in Wenling, China, studied in Beijing, moved to London where she learned English and began to write novels and make films, and has lived as well in Paris and Berlin.

How does one classify such writers? Is Lahiri an American writer? A South Asian diasporic writer? How are we to categorize her writing in Italian translated into English? Her fiction is set in both India and the United States, often focusing on issues related to migration, displacement, and the perpetual struggle of coming to terms with cross-cultural identity, topics that identify her work less with America or India than with the global conditions of displacement and migration, and with the fluidity of identity and cultural belonging associated with mobility. Hemon is both Bosnian and American, and, like Lahiri's writing, his moves back-and-forth between the two countries (and around Eastern Europe) in ways that belie rootedness in either place. It would betray something essential to his work as a writer to categorize him either as an American or a Bosnian writer. His writing, like much of the work discussed later in this book, focuses less on fixed national identities, and experiences rooted in a single country, than it does on the struggle to manage overlapping identities tied to multiple, intersecting locations and historical and cultural circumstances. This is certainly true of Mohsin Hamid as well, whose work is set in places as disparate as those in which he has lived, and therefore defies categorization along national lines as either Pakistani, American, or British. *Exit West*, like much of Lahiri's and Hemon's work, focuses on displacement, migration, cross-border experience, and the plight of refugees (the main characters in his book travel from an unnamed country, probably in South Asia, first to Greece, then to London and California). We will see later that the same holds true for transnational poets and dramatists working in places as disparate as Jamaica, Britain, China, Uganda, India, and, perhaps more importantly, in diasporic communities and arrival cities around the globe.

The challenges associated with categorizing writers like Lahiri, Hemon, and Hamid apply to nearly all of the writers discussed in this book, the great majority of whom are interested in transnationality because they are themselves transnational individuals, less rooted to a particular place than they are to mobility itself. They are interested as much in displacement as they are in belonging, and in focusing their literary writing on the challenges that displacement and mobility produce for developing a sense of home and belonging. It is tempting to think of these writers in terms of the notion popularized by the literary critic Homi Bhabha, who argues that those with mobile or hybrid identities occupy a third space, or a space between the double or triple identities they might lay claim to. However, there may in fact be no such space. The problem is that a "between" or "third" space denotes a kind of fixed and bordered place, but most of the writers discussed here live in and write about overlapping places both real and imagined, about characters who must live simultaneously with deeply internalized cultural traditions while at the same time assimilating new ones. Both they and their characters are shaped by competing notions of ethnicity, race, and nationality grounded at once in their home countries and those where they have found themselves having to start their lives over. It is no wonder, then, that we have come to find the notions of "British," "American," "French," and "German" literature, the conventional and overly neat and tidy national boxes in which we are used to placing writers, increasingly outdated. It is no wonder that the idea of transnational literature has come to seem so relevant in an age dominated by the provocative, disruptive, promising, and terrifying forces of globalization. Which is simply to say that transnational literature is, increasingly, the literature of our own time, a time marked by the profoundly uneven forces of decolonization, globalization, postmodernity, and electronic technologies, forces that have simultaneously created possibility and havoc, order and chaos, and which have pitted the romantic ideals of global citizenship against the dark violence of resurgent nationalisms.

What we are coming increasingly to see, then, is that the home country of an author does not necessarily mark the boundaries of their work, and provides only a partial rational for categorizing it. Our interest in the lives of others different from ourselves, especially those from formerly marginalized and colonized countries struggling to give voice to and tell stories that provide a counter-narrative to those which have proliferated in the West, which registers in the global popularity of many of the writers discussed throughout this book, has converged with electronic technologies of production and circulation in ways that have overwhelmed the traditional borders of both literary production and its study. The story of contemporary literature, whether seen from a Western or a non-Western perspective, is not so much the story of how national literatures have incorporated a new wave of minority writers (as important as that story is), but rather, how writers from regions of the globe that hardly ever counted in serious discussions of Literature (with a capital "L") have come to dominate contemporary writing.

The complicated ways in which mobility, situatedness, home, and belonging are treated by writers like Ghosh, Lahiri, Hemon,

Gappah, Hamid, and Guo, is exemplified by Caryl Phillips in his book, *A New World Order* (2001). Born in the Caribbean, raised in Britain, and a some-time resident of the United States, who would like his ashes scattered in the middle of the Atlantic, Phillips in many ways represents the quintessential, mobile, transnational writer. *A New World Order* collects essays devoted to the United States, Africa, the Caribbean, and Britain. Each section begins with brief recollections of Phillips' own departures and arrivals in each of these places. The first recalls his arrival in an airport in sub-Saharan Africa. Phillips is 32 at the time, and of African descent, but he has never been to Africa. Emerging from the terminal he writes that "I recognize the place, I feel at home here, but I don't belong. I am of, and not of, this place" (1). What gets fore-grounded here is the paradoxical experience of feeling at home but not belonging there, arriving in a new place that seems familiar and yet at the same time feeling displaced. Africa is home in the sense that his family line can be traced back to Africa (he was born on the island of St. Kitts in the Caribbean), yet not home because he was raised in Britain. "Recognize" in this passage has an imprecise, floating significance that isn't quite pinned down. Does he recognize the trappings of airports everywhere? Images of Africa he's seen in the media or read about in books? Or, is the sense of recognition here meant to refer to something deeper, something cultural, even something in his blood? It is not so much that he cannot pin down whether he is "of" or "not of" this place, but rather, that his identity is rooted (routed as well) quite precisely in his being both of and not of Africa.

The second flight he recounts, made 12 years earlier, is from Britain to the United States. The details of this flight are different than those of the flight to Africa, but the arrival is fashioned to match it: "I should be frightened and disoriented. But I am not. I recognize the place, I feel at home here, but I don't belong. I am of, and not of, this place." The recognition Phillips registers here is surely grounded in his having spent the first 20 years of his life growing up in London. For this reason, he is familiar with the look and feel and busyness of the metropolitan West. But his otherness also makes him not of this place. Born in the Caribbean and of African descent, Phillips is both at home and yet not at home in the West. The third flight he recounts is with his mother to

St. Kitts at the age of 22. Here he registers his arrival at a place where the sense of home will be more literal. Where Phillips' description of the first two arrivals has to do with shuffling passports, vaccination certificates, pushing luggage into bins, and finding taxis, this one features his mother's attempt to "compress everything into one short flight," to "explain a whole life in twenty minutes," to "repair inaccuracies, give information, to confess" (3). But Phillips' attention is riveted to the landscape below, the one out of which he was born:

> The plane is descending to the past. I look out of the window. Tall sugar cane sways in the breeze. I note a thousand different shades of green. Roads snake carefully between neat, manicured fields. Cars trickle. A church. A town square. A cluster of houses carelessly thrown together. A child's play town. I look across at my mother. There is much history still dammed up inside her.
>
> (3)

The focus here is on a descent not just from the air to the ground but into the past, into the history still dammed up inside of his mother. It puts the emphasis on St. Kitts as a kind of home different from Africa, Britain, or the United States, a home with a history leading back to Africa, but one formed as well out of the stuff of the island Phillips observes as he lands, and shaped by the Western-inflected perspective through which he views it. But that perspective also has deep historical roots, connected as it is both to the middle passage and to the local world evoked by the island's shades of green, manicured fields, and town squares. The description of his landing at St. Kitts ends with the same words that concluded the previous sections: "I look now at the island of my birth. I recognize the place, I feel at home here, but I don't belong. I am of, and not of, this place" (3).

From here Phillips turns to a series of anecdotes about the early years of his life as a young child in London, especially the challenges of navigating the fraught racialized world he encounters there, at school, walking down a street, at the cinema where he stands to sing "God Save the Queen," or attending a dance class. "I am seven years old in the north of England," he writes,

> too late to be coloured, but too soon to be British. I recognize this
> place, I feel at home here, but I don't belong. I am of, and not of, this
> place. History dealt me four cards; an ambiguous hand.
>
> (4)

This final repetition of the refrain about being at home but not belonging, about being both of and not of a place, underscores once again the paradoxes that form his identity, but with the added point that it is history that has created the palimpsest of his identity, his subjectivity. He is a simultaneous historical subject of Africa, the Caribbean, Britain, and the United States, subject to each country's social and cultural expectations and norms, at home in all of them and yet in none of them. Each place in its own way subjects him to its own racialized regimes of belonging, rendering his identity an ambiguity.

As a writer, Phillips tells us, he was formed by reading the work of other writers "who have been dealt the same ambiguous hand" (4), among them Frantz Fanon, James Baldwin, and the South African novelist, John Coetzee. The links he feels to these writers have been formed by his experience of racial otherness, and through the experience of migration and displacement recounted in the previous sections of the introduction. He goes on to underscore how these experiences have fitted him for "a twenty-first-century world. A world in which it is impossible to resist the claims of the migrant, the asylum seeker, or the refugee" (5). In his view, the "old static order in which one people speaks down to another, lesser, people is dead. The colonial, or postcolonial, model has collapsed. In its place we have a new world order," and "in this new world order nobody will feel fully at home" (5). "These days," he insists, "we are all unmoored," "our identities are fluid. Belonging is a contested state. Home is a place riddled with vexing questions" (6).

The kind of displacement Phillips evokes in these passages might seem like something distressing, a problem to surmount. Yet, the introduction to the section of essays about the Caribbean in his book bears the title "The Gift of Displacement." What is Phillips getting at here? In what sense does he think of displacement as a "gift?" He points out, to begin with, that in the Caribbean nearly everyone is displaced, its native peoples (the Tainos, etc.), their European colonizers (from Britain, Spain, Portugal, and elsewhere), the slaves they brought in chains from Africa, and the South Asian indentured servants who followed them. Migration in all these forms is the mechanism by which the Caribbean came into being, the point of departure for its very nature as a region. For this reason, "cultural hybridity" is "the quintessential Caribbean condition" (130). The value of the Caribbean, for Phillips, lies in its "migratory condition," and the sense of "displacement" it both depends upon and fosters (131). It is this knowledge of the migratory condition, this nearly inborn facility for managing displacement, that Phillips insists has been "a gift to the creative mind" (131) for Caribbean writers from Frantz Fanon and Aimé Césaire to V.S. Naipaul, Derek Walcott and Louise Bennett. More importantly, Phillips sees the twin gifts of having been born out of migration and thus having developed a facility for managing displacement as a kind of model for managing twenty-first century life in an increasingly globalized, transnational world:

> The truth is, it could be argued that the synthesizing new world vision of the Caribbean provides the perfect model for the age in which we live. An age in which migrations across boundaries are an increasingly familiar part of our individual lives as national borders collapse and are redrawn. An age in which nations bind together in regional clusters and eliminate old immigration laws, and in which illegal movements from one country to another become increasingly desperate as economies fail and wars continue to rage. How do we explain our new hybrid selves without recourse to the simplistic discourse of race? Perhaps the answer is to be found in the culture and literature of the Caribbean archipelago.
>
> (132)

For Phillips, the gift of displacement for the Caribbean is that it does not know the tyranny of purity ("the shadow of purity does not extend far south beyond the Florida Keys," he insists [133]), but rather, models synthesis and hybridity. Migration and displacement have worked together there, in his view, to create a kind of "cross-cultural fluidity," a "creolising Caribbean consciousness" that has "created a culture that is distinct from that of the United States, and certainly light years removed from that of Europe" (133–4). For all of these reasons, Phillips sees it as a kind of model for the twenty-first century. The identities he has had to juggle, the literal and cultural borders he has had to negotiate, the overlapping spheres of experience he has had to reconcile, link him to the generation of writers Ghosh identifies with, and their work, collectively, helps to add substance to our understanding of what constitutes transnational literature.

What makes transnational literature transnational, then, and what distinguishes it from world literature, is its sustained and wide-ranging engagement with cross-border experiences that transcend state borders and national identities, and its focus on the economic, cultural, environmental, and technological forces reshaping late modernity globally. The stories it tells, like those embodied in the sketches by Phillips discussed above, about travel, migration, and flight, and about the uneven effects of the forces transforming global modernity, focus attention on the alternatingly liberating and disruptive effects of mobility of all kinds—demographic, cultural, technological, informational, and economic. While these forms of mobility (or to recall Phillips' word, displacement) have always played a key role in human experience, they have accelerated in the twentieth and twenty-first centuries under the effects of decolonization and the economic, political, technological, and cultural forces of globalization.

For this reason, as we will see in Part II of this book, contemporary literature has become increasingly characterized by an engagement with the experience of the migrant and the refugee, with people who have embraced new forms of mobility as a way to escape poverty, war, and injustice, or who have become displaced by these forces. Some are forced to flee their homelands; others leave by choice to pursue educational and economic opportunities abroad. Some never return home, while others travel regularly back-and-forth between new homes and old, negotiating the cultural borders that divide them in increasingly nuanced ways. They bring with them perspectives that challenge a range of Western narratives—historical, political, economic, cultural, and religious. And they explore the experience of conquest, slavery, genocide, cultural extermination, and the history of nation-building from the point of view of those who have been victimized by those forces. In so doing, they challenge deeply entrenched historical notions of Western privilege, and develop critical explorations of the impact of racial assumptions regarding white, Western superiority, countering fantasies of purity with the realities of hybridity and syncretism.

At the same time, transnational literature pays particular attention to the broader technological, infrastructural, economic, and political developments that have, over the course of the twentieth and twenty-first centuries, made nation-state borders increasingly easy to navigate. Airports and railway stations, and the travel they facilitate, for example, play a prominent role in many of the literary works discussed in this book. So do border stations and border crossing facilities, and the bureaucratic structures they house. The Internet, Internet cafes, computers, cell phones, and the forms of instantaneous communication they facilitate, are also ubiquitous in transnational literature. References to multinational corporations, NGOs, globalized investment banking, human rights organizations, and colleges and universities educating an increasingly diverse, global population of students, abound. Transnational novels, poems, and plays interweave the daily lives of migrants, refugees, foreign students, bankers, international lawyers, and NGO operatives, all of them negotiating in their own ways these technological, bureaucratic, and institutional structures. And, of course, the plot of nearly every book, story, poem, or play discussed here unfolds in the context of political power, the historical and ideological shape of which is explored in nuanced and often subtle ways. And finally, the omnipresent threat of global terrorism, religious, fundamentalist, nationalist, racist, is a persistent subject of many of these texts.

It might seem that the subjects outlined here are the stuff of the social and political sciences. What role does literature—and its study—play in understanding globalization, decolonization, the plight of refugees and migrants, climate change, or the impact of technology on the reshaping of the nation-state? Aren't these issues best understood through the study of history, economics, political science, and sociology? Aren't questions about how to manage hybrid identities—a key topic in transnational literature—the purview of psychologists? And, isn't culture—its nature, function, and mutability—something anthropologists are best equipped to study? Such questions, of course, intersect with larger contemporary debates about the so-called "politicization" of the humanities in general, and of literary studies in particular. Beginning with the culture wars of the 1980s and 1990s, many observers have lamented the steady rise in interest among literary scholars and critics in literature's engagement with race, class, gender, psychology, political ideology, culture broadly defined, and sexuality, and the expansion of the canon that has come with it. They have lamented what they claim is an increasing lack of attention to literature's formal and aesthetic qualities, the critique of canonical works by critics who have focused attention on the circulation in those works of troubling political, social, and cultural ideologies, and a new, more representational and geographically diverse approach to the canon. Others, of course, have defended these changes as both a necessary and salutatory response to the historical insularity and narrowness of the canon in particular, and literary studies in general. This is not the place to rehearse these debates, let alone to adjudicate them. However, there are a few key points that ought to be made here, all of which have to do with the simple fact that literature has always been engaged with political, cultural, and social issues. Literary works have always foregrounded competing political and cultural ideologies. They have always explored class and its relationship to power, and have dramatized power relations in terms of gender as well. And finally, literary works have always been interested in the pros and cons of nationalism, and with the impact of economic and bureaucratic infrastructures on the lives of its characters. One form of politicizing literature is to ignore its treatment of these topics in the interest of focusing solely on its aesthetic characteristics. To marginalize or ban altogether the discussion of the political dimensions of literary works is itself a political act.

In fact, the aesthetic and the political are inextricably intertwined. The most compelling literature draws in new and original ways on the full range of aesthetic resources available to short story writers, novelists, poets, and dramatists in order to illuminate human behavior in its individual, social, cultural, and political dimensions. For this reason, it is a fundamental mistake to draw a distinction between the art of literature and its subject matter. The best literature is aesthetically sophisticated and intellectually and politically engaging at the same time. Political and historical novels that engage entrenched and conflicted ideologies can be artistically complex, even brilliant, and there is no reason why a beautifully told love story, poem, or play cannot be a vehicle for exploring history, politics, and power. Indeed, many of the literary works discussed in this book—about people in exile, about migrants, refugees, and people displaced by war and poverty—explore the pros and cons of nationalism, cosmopolitanism, globalization, purity, hybridity, and a host of other topics through the lens of deeply personal, intimate, romantic relationships. It is in the context of such relationships, in fact, that their volatility becomes most dramatic, and where what is at stake becomes so clear. And, as we shall see, they achieve their clarity by employing a wide range of innovative literary techniques in modes that run from the poetic and the lyrical to the prosaic and the dissonant, drawing on complex and sophisticated formal and narrative structures to weave together the stories they tell and the emotions they evoke.

For this reason, the discussion of transnational literature in Part II pays balanced attention to both the subjects and the artistic qualities of literary works, and to the intersection in them of the political and the intimate. Indeed, the formal structure, narrative technique, poetic diction, and theatrical staging in the works under discussion here all play a key role in shaping their intellectual and critical power. While the social sciences have an indispensable role in our understanding of the subjects and issues explored in transnational literature, there is no substitute for what the artistic perspective of a literary treatment can add to this understanding. Literature is free to develop perspectives and to take risks social science writing cannot. It can fashion complex plots, interweaving the many dimensions of contemporary global modernity into narrative or dramatic forms that tell the same story from different, often conflicting perspectives. Perhaps even more importantly, it has the uncanny ability to take us inside the heads of people, to dramatize their consciousness. No other medium has the power to put the reader inside the head of characters struggling with problems like theirs or a world away from anything they have ever experienced. Transnational literature draws on a myriad of narrative, linguistic, and formal devices in order to provide both intellectual illumination and emotional empathy regarding the plight of its characters and the shape of the world they are trying to negotiate, and a large part of the discussions that follow in Part II will focus attention on those devices.

FURTHER READING

Apter, Emily. *Against World Literature: On the Politics of Untranslatability* (New York and London: Verso, 2013).

Damrosch, David. *What is World Literature?* (Princeton: Princeton University Press, 2003).

Casanova, Pascale. *The World Republic of Letters*, trans. Malcolm DeBevoise (Boston: Harvard University Press, 2004).

Hitchcock, Peter. *The Long Space: Transnationalism and Postcolonial Form* (Stanford: Stanford University Press, 2010).

Hunter, Walt. *Forms of a World: Contemporary Poetry and the Making of Globalization* (New York: Fordham University Press, 2019).

Lionnet, Francoise, and Shu-Mei Shih, eds. *Minor Transnationalism* (Durham and London: Duke University Press, 2005).

Ramazani, Jahan. *A Transnational Poetics* (Chicago: University of Chicago Press, 2015).

Walkowitz, Rebecca L. *Born Translated: The Contemporary Novel in an Age of World Literature* (New York: Columbia University Press, 2015).

REFERENCES

Alighieri, Dante. *The Divine Comedy*, trans. Allen Mandelbaum (New York: Everyman's Library, 1995).

Anonymous. *The Epic of Gilgamesh*, trans. N.K. Sanders (New York: Penguin, 1960).

Anonymous. *The Mahabharata*, trans. John D. Smith (New York: Penguin, 2009).

Anonymous. *Tales from the Thousand and One Nights*, trans. N.J. Dawood (New York: Penguin, 1954).

Apter, Emily. *Against World Literature: On the Politics of Untranslatability* (New York: Verso, 2014).

Casanova, Pascale. *The World Republic of Letters* (Cambridge: Harvard University Press, 2007).

Dagnino, Arianna. "Transcultural Writers and Transcultural Literature in the Age of Global Modernity," in *Transnational Literature*, 4 (2), 2012. Retrieved at https://dspace.flinders.edu.au/xmlui/bitstream/handle/2328/25881/Transcultural_Writers.pdf;jsessionid=78B9BBFB9E145EF7F9F3F1E1D0629BE4?sequence=3.

Damrosch, David. *What is World Literature?* (Princeton: Princeton University Press, 2003).

Douglass, Frederick. *The Narrative of the Life of Frederick Douglass* (New York: Signet, 1997).

Gappah. Petina. *Out of Darkness, Shining Light* (New York: Scribners, 2019).

Ghosh, Amitav. *The Great Derangement: Climate Change and the Unthinkable* (Chicago: University of Chicago Press, 2016).

Goethe, Johann Wolfgang Von. *Faust: A Tragedy*, ed. Cyrus Hamlin, trans. Walter W. Arndt (New York: W.W. Norton and Company, 1976).

Goethe, Johann Wolfgang Von. "Essays on Art and Literature," ed. John Gearey. *Goethe's Collected Works*, vol. 3 (New York: Suhrkamp, 1986, 225).

Guo, Xiaolu. *Nine Continents: A Memoir In And Out of China* (New York: Grove Atlantic, 2017).

Phillips, Caryl. *A New World Order* (New York: Vintage, 2001).

Strich, Fritz. *Goethe and World Literature*, trans. C.A.M. Sym (London: Routledge, 1949).

Twain, Mark. *The Adventures of Huckleberry Finn* (New York: Penguin, 2003).

PART II

READING TRANSNATIONAL LITERATURE

INTRODUCTION
THE LAY OF THE LAND

Part I of this book sought to develop a comprehensive answer to two questions: What is transnational literature, and how has its study developed? In answering these questions, we explored the historical, social, and cultural forces that helped to shape both the emergence of transnational literature and approaches to its study. Here we shift to a discussion of representative works of transnational literature in fiction, poetry, drama, and creative non-fiction. However, this shift does not mean we are turning our attention away from the scholarly, critical, and theoretical concerns discussed in Part I. Rather, we will be exploring how the interests of transnational writers, and the scholars who study them, intersect with and inform one another.

As should be clear from our conceptual discussion of both "transnational" and "literature," the range of texts that could be discussed in this section is immense, much larger than could possibly be handled in a book of this size. For this reason, the discussion that follows focuses on transnational literature defined as a body of writing self-consciously engaged with transnational experience shaped by the combined forces of decolonization, postmodernity, technology, and contemporary globalization. Why? Put simply, readers interested in the broader category of world literature already have a wealth of scholarly, critical, and theoretical books on the subject to choose from, all supplemented by an array of anthologies containing examples of world literature from antiquity to the present. As we noted in Part I, world literature tends to be defined broadly, focuses on classical or great works from around the world, and is defined less by a set of subjects than by patterns of production, circulation, and reception. Beyond the deeply problematic claim that world literature deals with universal human experience, there are no particular issues or subjects with which world literature is concerned. Rather, the category seeks to emphasize the global range of literary production beyond the Western canon, and to highlight works from around the world that have had a particularly significant historical impact. As such, the field is an extremely important one. Transnational literature as we have been discussing it in this book, on the other hand, is a relatively recent phenomenon, the product of a particular set of late twentieth- and early twenty-first-century forces, literature that is specifically engaged with a range of issues—colonialism, decolonization, displacement, exile, migration, diasporic experience, globalization, and the explosion of electronic technologies—that have reshaped human experience in the wake of the Second World War. There is no body of work on this literature comparable to what exists for world literature.

Still, the category is immense, and the chapters that follow necessarily deal with a limited—but broadly representative—sample of transnational literature from regions where it has, for a number of historical reasons, proliferated: South Asia (in particular, India, Pakistan, and Sri Lanka), the Americas (including the United States, Canada, Latin America, the Caribbean, and Mexico), Africa (especially sub-Saharan countries like Nigeria, Zambia, and South Africa), Europe (from Britain and Germany to Poland and Bosnia), and the so-called Middle East (stretching from Egypt and the Sudan to Iraq, Iran, and Syria). Many scholars, as we have already seen, take this kind of regional approach to the study of transnational literature. Laura Doyle, for example, has encouraged literary scholars to develop a form of "'regional' transnational studies," a strategy that "focuses on the in-between" spaces of a more traditional approach oriented around the nation, one that works "across borders and yet within a certain circumference" ("Toward a Philosophy of Transnationalism," in *Locating Transnational Ideals*, 63). Focusing on "in-between" spaces means both paying attention to literature from regions of the world formerly marginalized in literary studies, and from those that cut across—or exist between—the borders of nation states, like those referenced above. We have already noted how this focus on regions has led to explorations of what Lionnet and Shih call "minor transnationalism," and to the proliferation of fields like border and island studies.

One particularly important example of this shift has been the recent focus on literature of the Global South, and the emergence of the term as a critical concept related to the study of the transnational impact of colonialism, decolonization, and globalization. The term "Global South," which became increasingly popular during the last three decades of the twentieth century, emerged as an alternative to more pejorative terms like "Third World" or "Developing Countries." It also came to be associated with a cultural and political position that highlighted the historical dominance of the Global North over the Global South, and with areas of study that developed both historical and contemporary critiques of that dominance. Thus, in literary and cultural studies, attention to literatures of the Global South (which includes Mexico, Latin America, Africa, the Middle East, Asia, Southeast Asia, and Micronesia) is not only an important example of the transnationalizing of literary studies. It also emphasizes the emergence of a literary imagination in these areas that uses the resources of poetry, fiction, and drama to explore a range of personal, social, cultural, economic, and political issues that extend across the borders of disparate countries.

Many of the texts discussed in the chapters that follow emerge from, or are connected to, the Global South. However, it is important to note that the term "Global South" is not simply a geographical marker. While the term does, of course, have a geographical orientation, the focus of Global South scholars on social and economic inequality there, and on how the forces of colonialism, decolonization, and globalization continue to shape the subjectivity and cultural consciousness of its people, means that work in this area deals both with marginalized and migrant populations from the Global South living in the North, and with privileged elites in the Global South. There is such a thing, that is, as a Global South diaspora dispersed across countries associated with the Global North, and in the Global South there are pockets of economically privileged populations who control both political power and economic resources (a subject that surfaces in a number of texts discussed below). To study literature about the Global South, then, involves not only reading texts written in the region, but also texts by migrant, exiled, or displaced writers from the Global South living and writing in the metropolitan centers of the Global North.

There are a few important caveats to be made about the other regions mentioned above, as well. It is important to stress the sometimes-overlooked fact, for example, that Africa is a continent, not a country, and that there are vast cultural and literary differences between, for example, Morocco, Egypt, Nigeria, Somalia, Zambia, and South Africa, to name just a few countries referenced in the literature discussed below. These countries share the experience of European conquest and colonization, yet the countries, languages, and literary traditions that subjugated the various regions of Africa—French, British, Dutch, Portuguese, etc.—are quite different. Because English has become a kind of lingua franca for transnational literature, its production has exploded in countries like Nigeria and South Africa, where English is a first language. The same is true, of course, of South Asia. Perhaps no country has produced the abundance of transnational literature, for this reason, as has India. This is, of course, one of the central paradoxes of transnational literature, that the language of colonial domination has been seized by writers from formerly colonized countries and used as an instrument for the critique in literature of that domination. The effects of globalization throughout the African continent, moreover, have been uneven at best, a fact reflected in much literature from the continent dealing with transnational forces. It is also important to keep in mind that the Caribbean, like Africa, is an incredibly diverse region of the world as well, made up of an array of island countries formerly colonized by the Spanish, British, French, and Dutch, populated by the descendants of those colonizers, slaves from Africa, indentured servants from South Asia, and a complex creole population that has proliferated in the wake of their intermixing, and among whom are writers working with a hybrid mix of literary traditions.

Also problematic is the designation "Middle East" for a huge swath of countries running from the western end of the Mediterranean Sea both east from Egypt across Saudi Arabia, Qatar, Oman, and Afghanistan, and north through Israel, Palestine, Iraq, Iran, Syria, Lebanon, and Turkey (a subject we will see treated in Marwa Helal's 2019 book, *Invasive Species*). The term "Middle

East" came into being only after the fall of the Ottoman Empire, and is actually a Western invention under the auspices of what was called the Sykes–Picot Agreement, which divided the former empire into British and French spheres. In the years after the First World War, much of what is now called the "Middle East" came under British control, including what are now Israel, Palestine, Jordan and Iraq. Many states now part of the Middle East did not exist until their borders were drawn by the French and British. As in Africa and the Caribbean, the nations of the contemporary Middle East are largely the invention of Europeans, and their borders papered over significant religious and ethnic differences (among Kurds and Turks, Sunni and Shiite, Christians, Jews, Igbo and Hausa, and Palestinian Arabs, for example), while creating spheres of British and French cultural influence.

The chapters that follow are organized in a way that foregrounds the general, overlapping subject they explore, and that emphasizes the stylistic and formal diversity of transnational literature. Chapter 4 explores the general interest in mobility among transnational writers, in a way that focuses both on the forms of travel, movement, and displacement treated in the literature, and on the literary devices, metaphors, and symbols used to evoke mobility. Chapter 5 highlights the treatment of borders and border zones in transnational literature, taking as its point of departure the distinction we observed earlier between literal and figural borders. While both Chapters 4 and 5 deal with mobility, travel, and displacement, Chapter 6 focuses in particular on the treatment of migration in transnational literature. Taking as its point of departure the treatment of migration and immigration in Hemon's and Gordimer's texts, it looks in particular at two novels that deal with North African immigration to Western Europe (Jenny Erpenbeck's *Go, Went, Gone*, and Helon Habila's *Travelers*) and the Egyptian-American writer Marwa Helal's dramatically complex treatment of citizenship, identity, belonging, and displacement in *Invasive Species*. Together, these texts employ a range of different literary devices in dealing with how the forces of decolonization and globalization have shaped twenty-first-century life. Chapter 7 picks up on the interest in identity not only in Helal's text, but in virtually all of the others discussed in the previous chapters. Taking as its point of departure Chimamanda Ngozi Adichie's discussion of authenticity in her TED Talk, "The Danger of a Single Story," it explores the complicated interrelationship between authenticity and identity (conceived in both personal and cultural terms) in transnational literature, first in an important story by Adichie, then in the Ugandan poet, Okot p'Bitek's "The Song of Lawino," and finally in Xiaolu Guo's *Nine Continents: A Memoir In and Out of China* (2017). These discussions are followed by sections on the treatment of identity by Jhumpa Lahiri in her short story, "When Mr. Pirzada Came to Dine," by Viet Than Nguyen in his novel, *The Sympathizer,* and in the poetry of the Jamaican writer, Louise Bennett. Chapter 8 again engages in a focused way with a subject that recurs in most of the texts discussed in previous chapters: history. History surfaces in transnational literature not only as a set of events but as an idea, and so this chapter looks at both the treatment of historical events, and the treatment of history as an idea or concept, in a range of texts by writers including Jhumpa Lahiri ("The Headstrong Historian"), Teju Cole (*Open City*), Junot Díaz (*The Brief Wondrous Life of Oscar Wao*), the Caribbean poet Derek Walcott (*Omeros*), and Laila Lalami (*The Moor's Account*).

While Chapters 4 through 8 focus on a mix of fiction, poetry, and creative non-fiction, Chapter 9 is devoted exclusively to transnational theater. Why? Because, as I explain at the beginning of the chapter, unlike the vast majority of fiction and poetry, the literature of the theater is meant to be performed live onstage before an audience. Plays exist—and circulate—in textual form, but they have their primary lives in performance. This is a particularly crucial distinction for the study of transnational literature, because the transnationality of drama is defined to a significant degree by the circulation of plays in performance. For this reason, Chapter 9 devotes a good deal of attention not only to critical discussions of some representative plays, but to a broader discussion of theatrical performance as a global phenomenon. This discussion includes not only the performance of dramatic texts, but of musicals and opera as well. Together they form a complex genre that, in the context of a discussion of the transnational nature of literature, deserves separate treatment. At the same time, it will be clear to the reader that virtually all of the subjects treated in the fiction and poetry discussed in earlier chapters receive sustained attention in transnational drama.

REFERENCES

Doyle, Laura. "Toward a Philosophy of Transnationalism," in Walter Goebel and Saskia Schabio, eds., *Locating Transnational Ideals* (New York: Routledge, 2010, 63–88).

Lionnet, Françoise, and Shu-mei Shih, eds. *Minor Transnationalism* (Durham and London: Duke University Press, 2005).

MOBILITY

No subject is more central to transnational fiction than movement, the voluntary or forced migration of people from one place to another, often through forbidding landscapes, with little or no money, across legal and cultural borders packed with hardship and promising little but displacement and the hope of a new beginning. Transnational stories, poems, and plays are full of journeys—on foot, by train, in the air—by people exiled or displaced, fleeing poverty, or religious, ethnic, or political persecution. Whether nomads, wanderers, exiles, or refugees, they are collectively in transition, negotiating legal and cultural borders in the face of dizzying complexities. However, while mass migration and the status of refugees have become pressing political problems around the globe, it is important to remember that migration has always been at the core of human existence. Indeed, Homo sapiens evolved out of Africa through migration, first into what is now Europe and the Middle East, and then into what is now India, southeast Asia, Australia, and eventually the Americas. Without migration, the human race would, in all likelihood, not exist as we know it. Seen from this perspective, migration is a natural process deeply linked to human evolution, and it long predates nationalism and the rise of nation-states. Human beings have always been in flight. And so, while the exploration in transnational literature of migration, displacement, travel, and journeys of all kinds, especially those that take place across increasingly permeable nation-state borders in the context of accelerating political, economic, cultural, and technological changes, makes them seem contemporary, they are actually hard-wired into human experience and are part of a very long history. Fueled by a range of contemporary forces—from the increasing ease of travel across borders in an age of accelerating globalization, to economic inequality and the flow of refugees displaced by ethnic, religious, and secular violence—human mobility and the demographic transformations that come with it have exploded in the late twentieth and early twenty-first centuries. In this chapter and the one that follows, we will look at how mobility in general, and migration in particular, have emerged as key topics in transnational literature.

FLIGHTS, OLGA TOKARCZUK (2018)

The ubiquity and centrality of mobility in human existence are the subjects of Olga Tokarczuk's strange and quirky novel, *Flights* (translated from Polish and published in English in 2018), which unfolds across a historical panorama in which nation-states, and their borders, play a very minor role. Tokarczuk's novel is a good place to start, not only to get a sense of the general importance of travel, mobility, and displacement as central subjects in transnational writing, but also to observe the range of formal and narrative devices that are often used to explore them: multiple intersecting stories that often unfold in a non-linear way and are narrated in different voices or from different perspectives; stories that are often linked less by plot than by subject matter, and which, more often than not, have a wide geographical sweep that works to call attention to connections between places that might seem very different.

All of the characters in *Flights*, to one degree or another, are nomadic, wanderers (indeed, the original Polish title of the novel, *Bieguni*, means "wanderers"). The English title signifies in a variety of ways, all of which are evoked in one way or another in the novel. Flight can, of course, refer to the act of flying, and so airports and air travel figure prominently in the novel. However, the word "flight" can also refer to escape through imaginative thinking, as in the phrase "flights of fancy." This sense of flight is linked, as well, to the act of "taking flight," fleeing from something threatening or dangerous, or just needing to get away. A flight can be something literal, and in this sense can be linked to travel in general, to a specific journey, to fleeing danger, or to being put to flight by war or the threat of war. In every sense of the word, "flight" implies movement, change, and displacement, and often signifies as well haste, disjuncture, the breaking of connections, and sudden change. Tokarczuk's narrative is about all of these effects, but it also employs formal and narrative devices that produce those effects in the reader. The novel itself is constantly taking flight as the narrative voice keeps changing, and extended plot lines are suddenly dropped in favor of short, one or two paragraph disquisitions on a particular topic (examples include "Wikipedia" on pp. 72–3, "A Very Long Quarter of an Hour," the entirety of which reads, "On the plane between 8:45 and 9:00 a.m. To my mind, it took an hour or even longer," on p. 118, and the four-line section on p. 226 entitled "Mobility Is Reality").

The disorienting effects of these formal and narrative disjunctions are enhanced by the book's sudden flights from one historical time period or geographical location to another. Nearly all borders in this book, between time periods, places, history, and fiction are fluid. There are narrative threads spread throughout the book that run from the seventeenth to the twenty-first centuries, and its locations include cities in Poland, Ukraine, and Western Europe, as well as Turkey and Africa. It also interweaves—without making any distinctions between them—stories based on purely fictional characters with others about historical figures such as Chopin's sister and the Dutch anatomist, Philip Verheyen. *Flights* is a book about flight which constantly takes flight. Disjunctive and fragmentary in form, its plots, its narrators, its locations, and its temporality are fluid and shifting. However, while the flights in its pages are abrupt and disorienting, the book itself is held together by its multifaceted focus on—and celebration of—mobility and change. Tokarczuk emphasizes this overarching preoccupation near the very beginning of the book when the narrator makes what will become a recurring claim about the central value of motion:

> Standing there on the embankment, staring into the current, I realized that—in spite of all the risks involved—a thing in motion will always be better than a thing at rest; that change will always be a nobler thing than permanence; that that which is static will degenerate and decay, turn to ash, while that which is in motion is able to last for all eternity.

(4)

And later, in a section enigmatically entitled "Everywhere and Nowhere," the narrator writes that

> whenever I set off on any sort of journey I fall off the radar. No one knows where I am .... I think there are a lot of people like me .... aware of their own instability and dependence upon places, times of day, on language or on a city and its atmosphere. Fluidity, mobility, illusoriness—these are precisely the qualities that make us civilized.
>
> (52)

This stress on the imperative of mobility, on the value of travel and change, even when it brings adversity, is ultimately connected to the fluid and disjunctive narrative form of the novel. This becomes clear in recurring sections on what Tokarczuk calls "Travel Psychology," ostensibly delivered by scholars at airports around the world (74). According to one lecturer, "Travel psychology studies people in transit, persons in motion, and thus situates itself in opposition to traditional psychology, which has always investigated the human being in a fixed context, in stability and stillness" (74). "A fundamental concept in travel psychology," this lecturer continues, "is desire, which is what lends movement and direction to human beings as well as arousing in them an inclination toward something" (75). The "foundational idea" of travel psychology, she continues, is "constellationality," which is the basis of "the first claim of travel psychology," according to which "it is impossible to build a consistent cause-and-effect course of argument or a narrative with events that succeed each other casuistically and follow from each other" (77). She insists that "in order to reflect our experience more accurately, it would be necessary instead to assemble a whole, out of pieces of more or less the same size, placed concentrically on the same surface. Constellation, not sequencing, carries truth" (77).

The difference between a structure based on linearity and one based on constellationality is that while a linear structure unfolds through a logical sequence of events that link characters in a cause-and-effect kind of relation, a constellation is a group or configuration of stories, characters, and topics related through juxtaposition. The contrast here between constellation and sequencing links the narrative form of the book to its subject. The privileging of motion over stasis has its corollary in the book's formal choice of constellation over sequencing, and so underscores how the narrative form of the novel is fitted to its subject matter. A constellation is an assemblage or collection of things organized to tell a story outside linear sequencing, and it is fitted particularly well to a novel that seeks not only to be about, but to embody and create, the disruptive experiences associated with mobility and change. Constellation is associated with discontinuity, narrative with continuity. Constellation operates in the novel through the thematic juxtaposition of otherwise unrelated events. The book's narrative voice, James Woods has pointed out, is like the novel's characters, "always on the move."

Appropriately, then, the novel is full of stories about vehicles of travel—cars, airplanes, ships, and trains—and to airports, train stations, hotels, guidebooks, maps, as well as to nomads (117) and pilgrims (122). It begins with a section title that suggests rootedness and stasis, "Here I Am," but very quickly the reader begins to encounter sections with titles like "Seven Years of Trips," "Everywhere and Nowhere," "Airports," "Returning to Routes," "Trains Are for Cowards," "Guidebooks," "Dr. Blau's Travels," "Home is My Hotel," and "Mobility is Reality," which punctuate the book and emphasize its focus on travel. Some of these sections, like "Travel Psychology" and "Dr. Blau's Travels," are threaded at regular points throughout the book and provide it with a hint of narrative continuity, however. One prominent example is the story of a Mr. Kunicki, whose wife and child inexplicably take flight from their car during a vacation. This story is told in three long sections, "Kunicki: Water (I)," "Kunicki: Water (II)," and, near the end of the novel, "Kunicki: Earth." Much time is spent recounting the family's journey, Mr. Kunicki's puzzlement at his family's sudden disappearance, and a subsequent police investigation. Although they eventually return, we never find out why they left in the first place.

Tokarczuk's approach to the subjects of travel, mobility, and displacement, then, is decidedly elliptical. This is partly the effect of the fragmented and disjointed form of the novel, which seems designed to alternately explore the psychic and the mundane aspects of travel, and to advocate for motion and change as a kind of bulwark against stasis and decay. The novel's interest in forms of flight of all kinds, with its lack of a coherent plot or narrative voice, and its absence of historical specificity, lends to its treatment of mobility a kind of conceptual or philosophical quality. It is not a novel about a specific form of mobility or travel, or about particular kinds of journeys related to personal, political, or historical circumstances. Rather, it is about the condition of flight per se, explored in a wide range of its iterations. This comes through especially in the "Travel Psychology" section, and others like it devoted to brief disquisitions that tend to philosophize on motion and change. There is, for Tokarczuk, something deeply fundamental, elemental, and essentially human about both, and this is one of the reasons why the novel's treatment of travel seems to be simultaneously focused and dispersed.

Tokarczuk's use of flight as a metaphorical device used to craft a novel about transnational movement across space and time—and her uncanny ability to enact that movement in the very structure of her book—is reflected in different forms in a number of other transnational texts. For example, Namwali Serpell's sprawling historical novel about colonialism, decolonization, and modernity in what is now called Zambia, *The Old Drift* (2019), uses the motif of drifting to conjure a different form of movement, less direct, more fluid, and with the inevitability of error built in. In addition, at regular moments throughout her narrative, a hive of mosquitos take over the story's telling, adding another metaphorical layer to the book's engagement with mobility and flight. Still later, mechanical drones enter the novel both to move along its plot, and to add technology to the mechanisms of mobility featured in the book. Serpell deftly uses these literary devices as a kind of supplement to reinforce her novel's larger preoccupation with the unfolding of colonial domination in Zambia, from the arrival there of the peripatetic David Livingstone to the history of formal British occupation and the arrival of settlers from Italy and India as well. A novel about exploration, colonization, migration, and displacement, the book underscores its focus on transit in all its various forms by utilizing a matrix of metaphors and devices.

OPEN CITY, TEJU COLE (2011)

Forms of flight, drifting, and mobility also provide a metaphorical framework for Teju Cole's novel, *Open City*, a complex transnational meditation on displacement and migration among Native Americans, the African diaspora, and Muslim refugees in New York and Brussels. Cole sets up his focus on human movement in a quick flurry of opening passages about bird migrations and radio waves. Bewildering upon first reading, this opening works subtly to set up the novel's engagement with human migration. Cole opens with a paragraph recounting the long, solitary evening walks the narrator, Julius, takes, "aimless wandering" (3) that sets the stage for Cole's focus on Julius as the contemporary embodiment of the cosmopolitan flâneur. But before we follow Julius out into the streets of Manhattan, his tendency to wander aimlessly is immediately connected to his "habit of watching bird migrations from my apartment," and he soon wonders "if the two are connected" (3–4). "I used to look out the window like someone taking auspices, hoping to see the miracle of natural immigration" (4). "Taking auspices" refers to the ancient Roman practice of reading omens into the patterns of bird migrations, and this fleeting reference to the flight of birds and the meaning it might hold sets up the book's focus on human migration as a natural process, and to Julius' preoccupation with interpreting—and coming to terms with his own involvement in—the history of human migration. This serves to encourage the reader to wonder whether Julius' own wanderings are really aimless, whether he is in fact himself in flight from something, and whether his own wanderings have a deeper meaning, whether they contain some kind of omen.

These opening passages on migration quickly cut to another reference to movement through the air, transnational radio waves carrying classical music broadcasts over the Internet "from Canada, Germany, or the Netherlands" (4):

> Pigeons flew by from time to time, as did sparrows, wrens, orioles, tanagers, and swifts, though it was almost impossible to identify the birds from the tiny, solitary, and mostly colorless specks I saw fizzing across the sky. While I waited for the rare squadrons of geese, I would sometimes listen to the radio .... I like the murmur of the announcers, the sounds of those voices speaking calmly from thousands of miles away .... Those disembodied voices remain connected in my mind, even now, with the apparition of migrating geese.
>
> (4–5)

The link here between the flight of migrating birds and the mur-muring, disembodied voices of the radio announcers on classical music stations around the world help set up the novel's sustained engagement with histories of migration and displacement, as we shall see in more detail in a later chapter. Cole's interest in move-ment and mobility, set up in the novel's opening pages with its focus on bird migrations and disembodied radio signals, is sustained by the novel's being structured around his peripatetic wanderings, both in Manhattan and Brussels, which serves to underscore his role as a contemporary version of the nineteenth-century flâneur. Because his cosmopolitanism is linked to his propensity to walk the city, he anticipates Tokarczuk's idealized vision of the link between civilization and mobility, driven by his own "instability" and "a dependence on place" and on "a city and its atmosphere," Julius' civilized cosmopolitanism is related to his "fluidity, mobi-lity" (Tokarczuk, 52). The upside of his cosmopolitan inquisitive-ness is that he leads the reader through the history of migrations and displacements that exist as a palimpsest beneath the surface of the cities he is in—from the traces of Native American footpaths to slave markets, African American burial sites, and echoes of the Middle Passage in Manhattan to the stories of North African migrants and refugees in Europe. The downside, however, is that Julius himself becomes so self-absorbed and turned inward that he fails to make human connection with others, or to take responsi-bility for his own actions. Deeply engaged with his own aesthetic experience—from classical music to folk art and New York City's architecture—he is at the same time estranged from his own con-nection to other members of the African diaspora there, with whom he clearly shares a kinship.

THE HUNGRY TIDE, AMITAV GHOSH (2004)

Amitav Ghosh also uses migration and flight as both literal subjects and literary metaphors to explore human, cultural, and ecological mobility in his novel, *The Hungry Tide*. Here it is the land itself that shifts and takes flight, grounding the novelist's exploration of human migration and displacement in a geographical space which is itself constantly migrating and shape-shifting: the Sundarbans, a delta region on the Bay of Bengal formed by the confluence of the

Ganges, Brahmaputra, and Meghna rivers as they empty into the bay. The Sundarbans are a natural and statutory border zone, comprising land that stretches across present-day India and Bangladesh. If liminality—the challenge of living, and carving out an identity in a place that is on the threshold where one space or existence is about to give way to another—is the larger subject Ghosh's book shares with those by Tokarczuk and Cole, then the Sundarbans are a material embodiment of that subject. The land becomes an extended metaphor of the ever-shifting boundaries between the people, cultures, and identities of the region, boundaries that have to be negotiated by the novel's main characters.

The plot of *The Hungry Tide* is centered on a handful of characters whose lives are in many ways at odds with one another. Kanai is a journalist returning to Lusibari, a village in the Sundarbans, where he grew up, to visit his mother. On the way, he meets Piya, a young Indian woman from the United States, coming to study dolphins in the same area. The boat she rents for her scientific work is owned by Fokir, a local, uneducated villager whose rustic ways contrast both with Piya's scientific orientation and Kanai's urban cosmopolitanism. Soon the book's chapters settle into a steady rhythm as they move back-and-forth between the story of Kanai's visit to Lusibari and Piya's search for dolphins with Fokir. Kanai carries with him a manuscript written by an older man named Nirmal, an activist, teacher, and writer who also lived in Lusibari and witnessed the Marichjhapi massacre, the forced eviction of 40,000 refugees (mostly Bangladeshi and Indian Dalit peoples) who had migrated to Marichjhapi Island in the Sundarbans. The history of the Marichjhapi refugees becomes the historical background for the present world Kanai, Piya, and Fokir are living in.

It is through Kanai's reading of Nirmal's notebooks (set off in italics) that the historical background begins to meld and intersect with the present. The liminal, mutable nature of the Sundarbans is emphasized early in the novel when Kanai reads a passage from Nirmal's notebook. In it, the Sundarbans are likened to

> *a heavenly braid ... an immense rope of water, unfurling though a wide and thirsty plain ... there is a point at which the braid comes undone ... washed apart into a vast, knotted tangle. Once past that point the river throws off its bindings and separates into hundreds, maybe thousands, of*

> tangled strands ... an archipelago, stretching for almost two hundred
> miles .... The islands are the trailing threads of India's fabric, the ragged
> fringe of her sari .... The rivers' channels are spread across the land like a
> fine-mesh net, creating a terrain where the boundaries between land and
> water are always mutating .... There are no borders here to divide fresh
> water from salt, river from sea.
>
> (6–7)

Like strands in the trailing thread of the rivers' channels, the past
and the present intersect, Kanai's cosmopolitanism is contrasted
with Fokir's folk wisdom, and Piya is pulled between the two of
them. Her Indian-American identity is already a puzzle to her, and
its shape-shifting matches that of the landscape. As an Indian she
appeared a foreigner in America, but as an American in India she
struck others, including Kanai, as a foreigner, and this of course
made her a kind of exotic in both places. This split in her identity
is emphasized at the outset of the novel—"she had no more idea of
what her own place was in the great scheme of things than she
did" of those around her in Lusibari (31)—a split embodied in her
being Indian/American, but doubled as well by her pull toward
both the rustic Fokir and the cosmopolitan Kanai, and between
her dedication to science, Kanai's to literature, and Fokir's to folk
wisdom and local mythology. Fokir, as a villager and expert boat-
man, becomes associated with the history of village life in Lusibari
and the Sundarbans and its rich mythology (which is both related
to and played off the poetry Kanai is enamored of). The longer
Piya and Fokir work together, the more her scientific expertise
becomes inflected by his reflexive knowledge of the water and the
dolphins, so that by the end of the book the borders between the
two have become productively interwoven.

OCULUS, SALLY WEN MAO (2019)

Ghosh's novel, especially in its focus on Piya and her efforts to come
to terms with her divided self—American yet Indian and in some
sense, therefore, neither—folds together an engagement with
mobility, displacement, and migration with the question of identity.
Fluidity, porousness, slippery borders, and shifting identities are all
linked in Ghosh's novel and, like Cole's, inform the complex web

of metaphors used to weave its various subjects together. The same thing can be observed in the poems contained in Sally Wen Mao's book, *Oculus* (Mao was born in Wuhan, China, and grew up in the United States). *Oculus* is the Latin word for eye, but the word is often used in its various forms to refer to seeing and sight. Iago, for example, provided "ocular proof" to Othello of Desdemona's supposed unfaithfulness, and the term oculus is often used in connection with camera lenses and circular openings that allow glimpses of light, such as the opening in the ceiling in Rome's Pantheon. Mao's title poem, "Oculus," about a young woman who commits suicide in Shanghai, invokes many of these meanings. It begins by referencing the act of opening one's eyes at waking, then mentions a "photo feed," the girl's "black eyes," "peepholes," "videos," how when the girl leapt to her death she was "awaiting a hand to hold,/ eyes to behold her as the lights clicked on," her "eyelashes all wet," her "windows ... curtain drawn," the "light in the night," and finally, how the girl "wiped her lens/before she died," and how "the smudge still lives."

Poetry, of course, and literature in general, is a kind of lens through which both writers and readers view the world. It can provide eye-opening glimpses into the material world, and into the psychological and emotional worlds of the characters it portrays, acting as a lens that can look out into the world, or deep within the psyche. Transnational literature, in particular, is a lens through which both writers and readers can explore other worlds, cultures, experiences, subjectivities, and ways of being in the world. Understood in this way, the ocular focus of Mao's book operates with special force in its poems about borders and boundaries (both literal and figurative, geographic and psychic), about liminality, travel, technology, identity, displacement, and our propensity for fetishizing others as exotic. This is particularly the case with regard to Mao's poems about China, which become occasions for her to explore the disparate, but linked topics of geography, empire, technology, travel, mobility, globalization, and identity. In so doing she offers a dramatic example of how poetry can imaginatively engage a variety of issues treated by transnational writers working in a range of genres. The best of them link history, geography, technology, and identity into a complex meditation on transnationalism and transnational experience.

"Antipode Essay," for example, although it is framed around ways of mapping geographical spaces, asks the reader to consider the challenges of having to link or reconcile antipodal (i.e. opposite) places, homes, cultures, and identities with one another, or, more precisely, how to inhabit the overlapping spaces they create. It is a poem about binary forces, and how they interact. Even the poem's title is relevant here, since the relationship between an essay and a poem is itself antipodal. The opening section, "Empire of Opposites," calls attention to the connections between what might otherwise seem like two very different things, geography and empire. In "popular myth," the speaker points out, "if you dig a hole in the Montana badlands/through the earth's private parts, your drill would end/up in China," where the poet was born. While, as the poem's title indicates, opposition itself is to be thought of as a kind of empire, Mao also gestures here toward the fact that, as a Chinese-born American, she is herself caught between two empires. The relationship between geography, empire, and identity explored in the poem is emphasized by the titles given to each poem's sections. Three of the poem's remaining sections (there are five) have Latin names referring to different ways to categorize land. Section II is called "Terra Nullis" (a territory that is not subject to the sovereignty of any state), section III "Terra Pericolosa" (a dangerous place), and section V "Terra Incognita" (a region that has not been mapped and thus has no identity). Section IV repeats the title of the first section, "Empire of Opposites."

"Terra Nullis" begins with a pun that reinforces the poem's interest in empire: "America cannot orient/itself without an opposite." The opposite empire, of course, is in the orient, China. While America's real, geographical antipode "is inhospitable ocean—all suds, spillage," Mao is calling attention to China as America's ideological antipode, and to the fact that nations, cultures, and empires tend to define themselves over against an imagined opposite. The poem at this point, of course, has an autobiographical element embedded in the tension it is exploring here, since Mao, born in China and now a citizen of the United States, is, as we have already noted, caught between two empires and thus two identities. "Terra Pericolosa" continues the focus on empire by stressing how "When two poles oppose,/west is the center and the rest/a suspect terrain," which is Mao's way of calling the reader's attention to how, for Western empires, the rest of the world, seen as uncivilized territory, is a "suspect terrain." "Empire of Opposites" finds the speaker "In Bogota, on my knees/with altitude sickness. Through the hostel window,/constant lightning." In the imagery of the window and the lightning the ocular is invoked once again, and it is followed by "eyes soldered," and an insistence by the speaker that "I'll take back my hemisphere, /my haute other-side."

While the poem begins in the badlands of Montana, it ends, in "Terra Incognita," with the speaker on a train that "galloped by Beijing." Thus, while the poem begins with the speaker in one empire, it ends with her in another. This traversal is emphasized at the outset of the section: "How democratic the stars were that night/the time we dug a hole/to America." But now the speaker is in a train passing by Beijing, and the train window offers up another ocular image: "Through the window I saw/the city's dust lift the plenum/of black hair." Here, the poem concludes, "the earth/was wet with heliotrope/and the sorries/buried underneath/couldn't sprout./If it rains enough, shame/may turn into seeds."

This poem is followed immediately by "Close Encounters of the Liminal Kind," which in narrative terms picks up from the conclusion of "Antipode Essay," since the speaker is on a train from Beijing to Wuhan. Moreover, the title's reference to liminality (a position at, or on both sides, of a threshold or border) recalls the prior poem's exploration of the speaker's position between opposite places and empires. However, it shifts attention away from nations, empires, and identity to a poetic meditation on twenty-first-century mobility, contrasting the high speed, magnetic Maglev train she is on with the modes of transport she had taken as a child in Wuhan: "I ride/the test track. We are crash test dummies/for levitation," carried on "magnetic/fields," speeding across China "without wheels." The subject of liminality comes into focus in the poem as the speaker becomes conscious of inhabiting a space between now and her childhood. As a child, the poet recalls, her family used to travel three to a seat, and outside of her window she glimpses a whole family cramped onto a single motorbike. "I watch them/from my porthole, missing/wheels, missing motion," missing "friction/against tracks," all of which makes her recall "the homes I've lost." This is soon followed by a reference to her increasing inability to recall or speak Chinese: "Sometimes I take weeks to remember/a single word in my own tongue ... I take hours to work/up the courage to ask a question."

This poem, following "Antipode Essays," evokes the extent to which modernity has increasingly become an empire of technology, a point reinforced more darkly by two other poems, "Electronic Motherland," which briefly references the 2012 riots at the multinational electronics plant, Foxconn, in Taiyuan, China, and "Electronic Necropolis," about workers in an electronic disassembly and recycling plant in Guiyu Village, China. The latter poem, about a factory where workers are regularly contaminated by the electronic parts they recycle, focuses on the ironic intersection between rebirth and death. It begins, "Behold how I tend to disappearance./By slicing open dead circuitboards,/I cultivate rebirth," dousing the electronic hardware in pyretic acid while "it scrapes me, enters me, a lather of data/against my organs, bless them,/my warring insides." Gutted hard drives lead to family ailments, "our sleep still short-circuiting," and the poem ends with a series of dystopian images of electronic parts, duress being unsoldered, "defects" that "supply/us with food, music, harm," all the while the polluted Lianjiang river "riven," a "bloodless organ," the "sum of foreign dross."

The subjects Mao covers in these poems—the complex interplay of geographic and ideological borders, the geopolitical tensions produced by competing empires, how identity gets worked out for people who live, simultaneously, in different, yet overlapping cultural worlds, the transformative effects of mobility, and the impact of new technologies on life around the globe—are recurring ones in transnational literature. What distinguishes Mao's poems, then, from the narrative fiction and theatrical works we discuss elsewhere? The answer to that question has to do with the nature of the poetic imagination—and of poetic language itself—how poetry as a literary mode has the power to compress into a quick and vivid sharpness detailed moments in the kinds of experiences both narrative and drama work out over many pages or scenes. Poetry, to come back to our discussion of the book's title, provides a special kind of ocular proof. If we follow the analogy of the photographic lens conjured up in the title and deployed in the poem "Oculus," then the novel is a wide-angle lens while poetry has a telephoto and a macro capability, able to zoom in closely on a single image, or part of an image. Take, for example, the opening line of Section II of "Antipode Essay," "America cannot orient/itself without an opposite," or the beginning of Section III, "west is the center and the rest/a suspect terrain." Whole essays have been devoted to these topics, and many of the novels discussed in this book are at pains to trace out their implications in long-form narrative. And yet, the combination of compactness and punning in these few lines has a kind of poetic power that fiction, for all of its value, has a difficult time sustaining. Poetry's poeticity is dramatically different from the discursivity of the novel or short story, and poetry opens us up to the kinds of complex mysteries found in phrases like "vampire meridian" or "hinterland of my blood" (which also come near the beginning of Section III of "Antipode Essay"). Only in a poem like this can the speaker "take back my hemisphere," a line that appears near the end of Section III, or where, in the poem's concluding lines, "shame/may turn into seeds."

Mao's use of the expressive power of poetry to explore mobility, empire, technology, and identity connects it to each of the novels discussed above. Indeed, both Tokarczuk and Cole have composed their novels in a kind of poetic idiom that helps to stress the links between poetry and narrative. There is, as well, a narrative element in many of Mao's poems, which serves the same function—to remind us of links between these genres, something we will explore in more detail later when we get to Derek Walcott's epic poem, *Omeros*. Before that, however, we will turn to a group of transnational texts in the next two chapters that deal more explicitly with contemporary issues surrounding immigration, migration, and the plight of the refugee, key topics in transnational literature.

FURTHER READING

Atta, Sefi. *A Bit of Difference* (Northampton: Interlink Books, 2013).

Aziz, Basma Abdel. *The Queue*, trans. Elisabeth Jaquette (Brooklyn and London: Melville House, 2013).

Dasgupta, Rana. *Tokyo Cancelled* (New York: Harper Collins, 2005).

Drndic, Dasa *Trieste*, trans. Ellen Elias-Bursac (Boston: Houghton Mifflin Harcourt, 2014).

Mater, Hisham. *The Return: Fathers, Sons and the Land in Between* (New York: Random House, 2017).

O'Siadhail, Michael. *The Five Quintets* (Waco: Baylor University Press, 2018).

REFERENCES

Cole, Teju, *Open City* (New York: Random House, 2011).

Ghosh, Amitav. *The Hungry Tide* (New York: Harper Collins, 2004).

Mao, Sally Wen. *Oculus: Poems* (Minneapolis: Graywolf, 2019).

Serpell, Namwali. *The Old Drift: A Novel* (London: Hogarth, 2019).

Tokarczuk, Olga. *Flights* (New York: Riverhead, 2018).

Woods, James. "'Flights,' a Novel That Never Settles Down." *The New Yorker*, Books, September 24, 2018, https://www.newyorker.com/maga zine/2018/10/01/flights-a-novel-that-never-settles-down

BORDERS

As we saw throughout Part I of this book, the treatment of borders and border zones in all of their various forms is a distinguishing feature of transnational literature and its study. While it is obviously the central focus of Border Studies, an engagement with borders, both literal and figural, is a key feature of virtually every transnational approach to the study of literature we have discussed. For this reason, it should hardly seem surprising that virtually all of the texts we explored in the last chapter are engaged in one way or another with borders. The dizzying array of stories and short riffs that make up Tokarczuk's *Flights* are a virtual compendium of cross border excursions of one kind or another, a fact that is underscored by the book's focus on "travel psychology" lectures delivered at airports extolling the virtues of mobility and the perpetual crossing of borders, all reinforced by the book's preoccupation with flight in all of its various manifestations. The book's locations, as well, move around between Poland, Ukraine, and Western Europe, as well as Turkey and Africa, and it is punctuated, as we saw, by references to hotels, train stations, airports, maps, guidebooks, pilgrims, and nomads. Cole's *Open City*, as we also saw, is preoccupied with the historical plight of displaced people who are moved by force or their own will across national, cultural, and personal borders of all kinds (this includes a range of populations of course, from native Americans to members of the African diaspora and north African refugees in Belgium). Ghosh's *The Hungry Tide* explores a world in which not only people but the land itself have to negotiate shifting borders, where clear distinctions that demarcate identity begin to blur. The forms of mobility his novel explores facilitate the same kind of crossing of borders that we find in Tokarczuk's and Cole's novels. The same is true with regard to the poems we discussed in Sally Wen Mao's *Oculus*, with its focus on "antipodal" locations, shifting empires, and disorienting train trips across China.

In all of these texts, borders and border zones are treated as paradoxical spaces, whether the term is applied to actual, nation-state borders, or more figuratively in discussions about identity and culture. As Alberto Rios notes in his poem "Border: A Double Sonnet" (2015), borders can be clearly demarcated and ephemeral, zones of exclusion and inclusion, ordered and chaotic, real and imaginary. For Rios, "The border is a line that birds cannot see" (l.1), "a real crack in an imaginary dam" (l.11). While the border used to be "an actual place," "now, it is the act of a thousand imaginations" (l.12). "The border says *stop* to the wind, but the wind speaks another language, and keeps going" (l.7). The border's ephemerality is matched by its double-edged nature: "The border has always been a welcome stopping place but is now a stop sign, always red" (l.9). "The border, the word *border*, sounds like *order*, but in this place they do not rhyme" (l.13). It "is the place between the two pages in a book where the spine is bent too far./ The border is two men in love with the same woman" (ll.16–17). The poem ends with the following lines:

> The border is mighty, but even the parting of the seas created a path, not a barrier.
> The border is a big, neat, clean, clear black line on a map that does not exist.
> The border is the line in new bifocals: below, small things get bigger; above, nothing changes.
> The border is a skunk with a white line down its back.
>
> (ll.25–8)

Rios' poem makes its point not just through the repetition in each line of the paradoxical and double-edged nature of borders, their simultaneous existence as real and imaginary spaces and as sites that create both order and disorder, but by its formal structure as well. While it is called a "double sonnet" and contains 28 lines, the border between the two sonnets it contains is invisible, with the two parts combined into one poem, for there is no formal, graphic, or thematic break between the first 14 lines and the second 14 lines. Structured in this way, the poem serves to emphasize the elusiveness of borders.

This chapter takes a closer look at the treatment of borders and border zones in two transnational novels, Nadine Gordimer's 2001 book, *The Pickup*, and Aleksandar Hemon's *The Lazarus Project*, published in 2008. Both of these books are particularly preoccupied with border crossings related to migration and displacement, but both engage questions of cultural difference and identity as well. The first half of Gordimer's novel is set in South Africa; the second in an unnamed country, probably in North Africa or the Middle East. As we shall see, this split divides the novel between two locations which represent both the literal and figural borders challenging the couple at its center. These locations are supplemented by various other micro-locations set off against one another—cities versus suburbs, villages versus the desert, etc.—that reinforce the novel's interest in what is involved in both the drawing and transgressing of borders. Hemon's novel also moves between two general locations, the United States and Eastern Europe, as its protagonist-narrator seeks to explore his own status as a refugee by cobbling together the story of another refugee who died nearly 100 years earlier. Hemon's book, like all of the other texts we have discussed so far, blends an engagement with literal borders and border zones—both as mechanisms that police and transgress difference—with explorations of figural ones as well related to culture and identity. Both books, finally, look at all of these issues through the lens of romance and intimacy, a device which helps serve to magnify what is at stake, personally, for the protagonists of each.

THE PICKUP, NADINE GORDIMER (2001)

Ghosh's novel explores the historical plight of refugees in the Sundarbans, the clash between tradition and modernity, and the challenge of conceptualizing identity in an increasingly globalized world, but at its heart is the romance plot involving Piya and Fokir. Strikingly, transnational literature about migration and displacement often fuses the personal and the political by threading its themes through romance. In the best of these books, the romance plot is not a distraction but in fact lends a deep urgency to the political, economic, historical, and cultural issues these books are pursuing. A good example is Nadine Gordimer's novel, *The Pickup*. In it, Gordimer also weaves location, landscape, migration, and human longing together in a novel that, like Ghosh's, deals with cultural and political issues through the lens of intimacy, and a romantic longing for the other. It is never quite clear who picks up whom in *The Pickup*.

Julie is a young, single white woman who has fled the bourgeois suburbs of Johannesburg for a life in the city center with a group of left-leaning intellectual friends, who meet regularly at the L.A. Café. She becomes romantically involved with Ibrahim (who goes by the alias Abdu through much of the novel) when her car suddenly breaks down in urban traffic. Ibrahim is an auto mechanic from an unnamed country in the Middle East who is in South Africa illegally, and, while Julie's growing flirtation with him seems to mark Ibrahim as the pickup, it increasingly becomes apparent it may be the other way around. The two become involved romantically at the same time that Julie is becoming estranged both from her wealthy family in the suburbs, and her smug cosmopolitan friends at the café. When the authorities track Ibrahim down and he has to leave the country, the couple marry and, midway through the book, Julie chooses to return with Ibrahim to his home village. At this point their roles are reversed. *Julie* becomes the displaced person, the cultural outsider, while Ibrahim chafes under the estrangement he feels from his family, as much a stranger in his home country as Julie had been in hers. Where a romance plot like this might seem to run the risk of trivializing the geopolitical, racial (Ibrahim is dark skinned), cultural, and economic issues Gordimer is writing about, that plot actually serves to intensify what is at stake.

Like Cole's New York and Brussels, Johannesburg is not quite as open a city as its diverse inhabitants might like to think. As Ghosh does in *The Hungry Tide*, Gordimer also invests the book's principal locations with symbolic import that helps shape, and pull into focus, the larger issues she is exploring. In Johannesburg, Julie's world is divided between the suburbs where her parents live, and the L.A. Café where she spends time with her friends. The Suburbs (always capitalized in the novel to underscore their symbolic import) represent a bourgeois world of financial power fueled by globalization. "An investment banker in this era of expanding international financial opportunities" (41), her father's garden parties are a carefully curated affair, the names on his guest list chosen pragmatically for "balance" (41). When Julie brings Ibrahim to meet her parents, the act is seen as "the latest wearying ploy to distance herself from her father" (41). "Their lives were always in control, these people," Julie thinks to herself, and "their reality did not know of his [Ibrahim's] existence" (42). At one point, there is an exchange about one of Julie's father's friends who is relocating for business reasons to Australia that captures Ibrahim's attention. "Was it easy to get entry?" he asks the man (46). "Nobody must laugh at this: the idea that a man of such means and standing would not be an asset to any country. The executive director of a world-wide website network" (46–7). The executive's mobility, of course, is in painful contrast to Ibrahim's. Later, Ibrahim looks up the English word "locate" to make sure he really understood the discussion:

> Locate: to discover the exact locality of a person or thing; to enter, take possession of.
> To discover the exact location of a "thing" is a simple matter of factual research. To discover the exact location of a person: where to locate the self?
>
> (47)

"To discover and take over possession of oneself, is that secretly the meaning of 'relocation' as it is shaped by the tongue and lips in substitution for immigration?" he wonders (48). The play here on location and relocation, and the focus on what for Ibrahim is the challenge of "where to locate the self," is telling, but it also drives home for the reader the novel's deep investment in exploring the relationship between location and identity, and how class (and race) enhance or limit transnational mobility. Julie has the luxury to flee the moneyed, bourgeois identity associated with the Suburbs, but Ibrahim has no such freedom. While the immigrants moving to Australia are being celebrated by their friends, Julie, aware of the painful irony of all this for Ibrahim, "is seeing the couple as those—her father's kind of people—who may move

about the world welcome everywhere as they please, while someone [like Ibrahim] has to live disguised as a grease-monkey without
a name" (49).

Gordimer pointedly contrasts the world of the Suburbs with the
urban, liberal cosmopolitanism of the L.A. Café where Julie hangs
out. Situated in "a bazaar of all that the city had not been allowed to
be by the laws and traditions of her parents' generation" (5), the L.A.
Café is a place where "the inhibitions of the past" are "breaking up"
(5). Full of people "haphazard and selectively tolerant," it is "a place
for the young," but also "where old survivors of the quarter's past,
ageing Hippies and Leftist Jews, grandfathers and grandmothers of the
1920s immigration who had not become prosperous bourgeois, could
sit over a single coffee," mixing with "crazed peasants" from the
"rural areas" and "prostitutes from Congo and Senegal" (5–6). Her
friends are not shy about asking Ibrahim who he is and where he
comes from, but the narrator bitingly dismisses this as "just the reverse
side of bourgeois xenophobia" (14). Once they find out where he is
from (though the reader never does) they quickly caricature the place:
"no development, what can you grow in a desert, corrupt government, religious oppression, cross-border conflict—composite, if
inaccurate, of all they think they know about the region, *they're* telling *him* about his own country" (14).

On the one hand, the Suburbs represent entitled, white, bourgeois prosperity fueled by economic globalization, and on the
other, the L.A. Café represents a site of resistance and rebellion
against the norms and traditions associated with them. It might
seem easy for the reader to choose sides, but something more
complicated and troubling is being played out in the space
between these two places. Gordimer goes out of her way to make
the cosmopolitanism of the L.A. Café crowd seem smug and dis-
tasteful, self-serving and simple minded, hardly a comfortable
refuge for Ibrahim. And perhaps more importantly, the Suburbs,
loathed by Julie and her friends, prove attractive to Ibrahim.
"Why," he asks her, "do you choose those friends. Instead of your
family" (62). Julie is puzzled, and Ibrahim explains that, from his
point of view, the group in the Suburbs "are people doing well
with their life. All the time. Moving on always. Clever. With what
they do, make in the world, not just talking intelligent" like Julie's
friends at the L.A. Café (62). Julie's father's friends "know what

they speak about. What happens. Making business. That's not bad, that is the world. Progress. You have to know it. I don't know why you like to sit there every day in that other place" (62).

"Place" and "location" are key words in the passages being discussed here, and Gordimer has deftly challenged the reader's expectations of what these specific places—the L.A. Café and the Suburbs, are meant to represent. On the one hand, she wants us to understand the key connection between location and identity, the ways in which identity is subject to location and place (which is why the term "subjectivity" has come to replace identity in contemporary discussions of the self). This serves to foreground the importance of displacement, in both its negative and positive senses. Ibrahim has become displaced in Johannesburg, and Julie in the Suburbs, and that displacement defines their identities. Julie has relocated to the urban center, its liberalism represented by the L.A. Café crowd, a move that reifies a new identity she's trying to shape. However, the kind of relocation offered by economic prosperity and embodied in the group at Julie's father's party, seems more substantial to Ibrahim. The significance of what Gordimer is exploring is important to understand. She is moving beyond simply vilifying the Suburban crowd as, in effect, responsible for Ibrahim's plight, and valorizing the L.A. Café crowd for their dissident resistance to them, and their embrace of Ibrahim. She wants the reader to see how both groups can be read that way, but she also wants us to see that Julie's complicity in the smug, self-serving, idealistic liberal talk has more to do with making her and the L.A. Café crowd feel good about themselves than it is about actually getting to know Ibrahim and helping him out. In his view, the group in the Suburbs get things done. They have power and authority, and that is what he lacks.

All of this means that *The Pickup* is simultaneously about the plight of displaced immigrants like Ibrahim, and those like Julie in developed countries that seek to help them. This becomes clear in the second half of the book when Julie and Ibrahim, having married, return to his small village on the edge of a desert. This abrupt shift in locations means that the couple have switched roles. Julie is now the displaced Other, making her way in a place and cultural world she knows little about. Here the desert at the edge of the village takes over the key symbolic role played in the first half of the book by the Suburbs and the L.A. Café. Early in their relationship in Johannesburg Julie remarks on how wonderful the silence is when they're together, a precious commodity in the big city. However, Ibrahim has exactly the opposite reaction. "To him this was not silence, this lullaby of distant traffic she took for it! Silence is desolation; the desert" (34). "Round the village?" Julie asks (34). "Everywhere," he responds, "as soon as you walk some steps, some few yards from our house" (34).

This is, of course, precisely the spot Julie is drawn to once she relocates to Ibrahim's village, and her fascination with it is a measure of how they are moving in diametrically opposed directions in spite of their deep intimacy with one another. "Where the street ended, there was the desert .... It was bewildering to her: come to a stop. At the end of a street there must be another street" (131). In her experience, "a district leads to another district," but here, "everyday suddenly ends" (131). She returns again and again to this spot as if somehow her shifting sense of self is grounded here and defined by the wide immensity of nothingness that fixates her. Returning to the "sudden end of the street" later in the book, she is struck by the "immensity" of the desert, how it "put a stop" to everything familiar in the village—houses, people, street vendors, cars, and lights—replacing it in her view with "no horizon to be made out," "no fixed object," just sand that is "immobile" (167). The desert for Julie becomes a place "out of time," with "no seasons of bloom and decay," for "she is gazing—not over it, taken into it, for it has no measure of space, features that mark distance from here to there," the "desert is eternity" (172). The desert has become many things here for Julie: a world of total escape, a border between a world of urban discomfort and its absolute erasure, a symbol of the liminal position she finds herself in, and a place where time and sequence seem obliterated.

While Julie burrows ever more deeply into the kind of existential escape the desert seems to offer, Ibrahim, who "shuns the desert" because "it is the denial of everything he yearns for" (262), seeks refuge in a country that will provide them economic opportunity. Here the inequities in their situations become clear: Julie is white, and she can afford to experiment with her identity because she has her parents' money to fall back on, while Ibrahim, a poor, dark-skinned Muslim man, is unwelcome, if not suspect, almost everywhere he tries to go. Having come to South Africa on a permit that has expired, he has become illegal and has been deported. "There was a litany of countries he had tried that would not let him in" (19). Though he has a degree in economics, "I'll be a burden on the state, that's what they say. I'll steal someone's job, I'll take smaller pay than the local man" (19). While Julie visits the desert, and spends time with the women in Ibrahim's family, he applies "for visas for emigration to those endowed countries of the world he had no yet entered and been deported from. Australia, Canada, the U.S.A., anywhere, out of the reproach of this dirty place that was his" (137–8). Julie is free to travel and relocate anywhere but wants to stay in Ibrahim's village, while his desire to emigrate is restricted by his being a Muslim man and therefore suspected of having "possible connections with international terrorism," of being someone "fighting their own ideological battles on other nations' soil" (140). While Julie has the luxury to experiment with the Otherness the desert represents, Ibrahim and his young Muslim friends long for substantive political and economic change at home:

> These young men want change, not the rewards of Heaven. Change in the forms it already had taken for others in the old century, change for what it was becoming in this new one. To catch up! With elections that are not rigged or declared void when the government's opposition wins; hard bargains with the West made from a position of counter-power, not foot-kissing, arse-licking servitude ... change with a voice over the Internet not from the minaret, a voice making demands to be heard by the financial gods of the world ... bring the modern world to Islam but we're not going to allow ourselves to be taken over by it ... total Islamization—against world powers?—what a mad dream; no, no—we must cross-fertilize Islam with the world if the ideals of Islam are to survive.

> (176–7)

It is important to stress that Gordimer is less interested in endorsing any particular position among those laid out for the reader in *The Pickup* than she is in giving each of them an airing and putting them in conflict with the others. As a writer, she is operating with something like what the Romantic poet, John Keats, called *negative capability*, the capability to think about reality from different points of view without having to reconcile their contradictory aspects into a single, exclusive truth. Ibrahim's interest in the economic and social power of Julie's father's friends in the Suburbs does not negate the novel's implicit critique of economic globalization. Likewise, Gordimer's satirizing of the comfortable cosmopolitan liberalism of Julie and the crowd at the L.A. Café does not mean that cosmopolitan liberalism is always insincere and destructive. And, while the moderate position on Islam Ibrahim and his friends take seems wisely pragmatic, that does not necessarily undercut the legitimacy of more orthodox versions of Islam. The value of Gordimer's novel lies in the conflicts it stages between different points of view on issues central to the history of colonialism, decolonization, migration, citizenship, economic globalization, and the messy business of drawing legal, cultural, and even personal boundaries in an increasingly globalizing world.

Gordimer's novel focuses on the overlapping stories of Julie and Ibrahim in order to foreground the conflict between the idealism afforded by her privilege and the pragmatism necessitated by the realities driving his predicament. He longs for the economic comfort and social stability she is seeking to escape. They live in a world, at the beginning of the twenty-first century, in which the histories of colonialism, globalization, and decolonization have converged both to upend their lives and create new possibilities. Disruption has bred possibility for both of them—the possibility of intimacy together, the possibility for Julie to break from what she finds to be the stultifying economic and cultural world her parents inhabit, and the possibility, for Ibrahim, of breaking free from postcolonial paralysis in his own country. The irony, as we have seen, is that the system of economic globalization that seems to offer him hope is the very system Julie is seeking to escape. And, of course, Ibrahim's possibilities are circumscribed by the contemporary geopolitics of Islamophobia, something that only affects Julie by virtue of her having married him. Gordimer is careful to make clear that the whole weight of history has shaped their predicaments. On Julie's side, the sense of guilt that comes from having inherited the privileges afforded by Dutch and British colonialism in South Africa, fueled by its administration of an apartheid state and supplemented by her father's success in the system of global finance. On Ibrahim's side, which is the *other* side, is the history of colonial domination, the difficult tension under decolonization between Islamic fundamentalism and a more secular state, and the onus of trying to immigrate to the West during a time of escalating religious, cultural, and political conflict. While Julie gives Gordimer the opportunity to interrogate the privileges of economic wealth and cultural cosmopolitanism in a world where transnational connections of all kinds have accelerated, Ibrahim gives her the opportunity to explore the plight of the migrant in an age fueled increasingly by nationalism and xenophobia. Together, Julie and Ibrahim represent the border where these two worlds overlap and intersect.

THE LAZARUS PROJECT, ALEKSANDAR HEMON (2008)

Where Gordimer's novel explores the overlap between Julie and Ibrahim in order to foreground their differences, Aleksandar Hemon uses a similar device in *The Lazarus Project* to explore many of the same issues Gordimer is concerned with—displacement, cultural conflict, immigration, geopolitical conflict, all in the context of romantic entanglement—but toward a different end. Where the overlap between Julie and Ibrahim in *The Pickup* stresses how history has put them on two different, seemingly irreconcilable trajectories, the overlap between Brik and Lazarus in Hemon's novel serves to illustrate how lives lived 100 years apart can intersect in a way that calls attention to the terrifying banality of historical repetition. Hemon's novel is narrated by Brik, a Bosnian refugee living in Chicago who has set out to write a book about an actual historical figure named Lazarus Averbuch, an East European Jewish immigrant, who was shot and killed in March, 1908, by the city's Chief of Police, George Shippy. The novel opens with a fictionalized retelling of the actual shooting (Averbuch had come to Shippy's home for reasons that have never been clear, and he was shot dead in the entrance way). The next section opens with Brik writing about himself:

> I am a reasonably loyal citizen of a couple of countries. In America— that somber land—I waste my vote, pay taxes grudgingly, share my life with a native wife, and try hard not to wish painful death to the idiot president [George W. Bush]. But I also have a Bosnian passport I seldom use; I go to Bosnia for heartbreaking vacations and funerals,

and on or around March 1, with other Chicago Bosnians, I proudly and dutifully celebrate our Independence Day with an appropriately ceremonious dinner.

(11)

Brik explains later to a woman whose foundation he hopes will fund his writing that he stumbled on the story of Averbuch's shooting while doing research for a column he was working on for the *The Reader*, a local Chicago publication. Brik's fascination with Averbuch, but more importantly, his strange identification with him, will take up the rest of the book, as Brik's Lazarus project becomes Hemon's *The Lazarus Project*.

The structure of the novel is key to what is at stake in that project. It moves back-and-forth with a marked regularity between chapters about Brik, writing and researching his book in the first few years of the twenty-first century, and chapters about Averbuch in the first few years of the twentieth century, his life in Chicago, his youth in the city of Kishinev, where he and his family are subject to the horrors of the Jewish pogrom, and his flight from Kishinev as he makes his way across a series of borders to the United States and Chicago. The chapters about Averbuch are based on his life but at the same time wholly fictional, as Brik imagines scenarios and writes pages of dialogue between Averbuch and others he could not possibly have any knowledge of. The imagined nature of Brik's account of Averbuch is the point, since *The Lazarus Project* is a highly self-reflexive book (a quality it shares with much transnational literature). It is about its own writing, and is full of passages about the nature and function of storytelling, exploring the relationship between fictional and historical stories, journalism, and even photography. Here is how Brik describes the book he wants to write:

> I wanted my future book to be about the immigrant who escaped the pogrom in Kishinev and came to Chicago only to be shot by the Chicago chief of police. I wanted to be immersed in the world as it had been in 1908. I wanted to imagine how immigrants lived then. I loved doing research, poring through old newspapers and books and photos, reciting curious facts on a whim. I had to admit that I identified easily with those travails: lousy jobs, lousier tenements, the

acquisition of language, the logistics of survival, the ennoblement of self-fashioning. It seemed to me I know what constituted that world, what mattered in it. But when I wrote about it, however, all I could produce was a costumed parade of paper cutouts performing acts of high symbolic value: tearing up at the Statue of Liberty, throwing the lice-infested Old Country clothes on the sacrificial pyre of a new identity.

(41)

Brik's own self-fashioning is partly played out in the writing of his book as he follows the thread of his identification with the immigrant Averbuch through the connections that linked the genocide committed in the war in Bosnia to the genocide of the Kishinev pogrom, his own immigration to Averbuch's, and life in Chicago's Bosnian diaspora to life in its Jewish diaspora 100 years earlier. Raising this Lazarus from the dead seems the key to raising himself from the dead. The rest of the book unfolds as time gets reversed and stories get made up. Brik enlists his friend, Rora, to journey with him back to Ukraine and Kishinev, essentially retracing the path Averbuch, his sister Olga, and his friend Isador took in coming to America. The more Brik and Rora exchange stories about storytelling, the more imaginary Averbuch's story becomes, and the more absorbed *The Lazarus Project* becomes in the redemptive possibilities of writing about, and thus remaking, the past.

The challenge of Brik's project is to fashion a double-stranded narrative that can make sense of Averbuch's experience and his own, weaving together an imaginary narrative of Averbuch's life in order to fashion some kind of order for his own. Creating that order has a lot to do with fashioning a transnational identity, one that moves perpetually through, across, and ultimately beyond "Bosnian" and "American," not a third identity so much as one that is simultaneously informed by both. The problem is that, for Brik, each of these national identities has become a kind of parody. Here he is writing about the party at which he and his "fellow double-citizens" celebrate Bosnian Independence Day:

[S]oon whatever meager Americanness has been accrued in the past decade or so entirely evaporates for the night; everybody—myself included—is solidly Bosnian, everybody has an instructive story about cultural differences between us and them .... Inevitably, over dessert,

> the war is discussed, first in terms of battles or massacres unin-
> telligible to someone (like me) who has not experienced the horrors
> .... In the official part of the evening, cultural diversity, ethnic toler-
> ance, and Allah are praised .... They dance, too, the kids .... No one in
> the audience has ever worn such clothes in their lives; the costumed
> fantasies are enacted to recall a dignified past divested of evil and
> poverty. I participate in that self-deception; in fact, I like to help with
> it, for, at least once a year, I am a Bosnian patriot.
>
> (12–13)

The inauthenticity of this collective faux Bosnian identity, and the repeated jabs at celebrating cultural diversity, are complicated by Brik's own sense of his being an inauthentic American. Here, for example, he recalls the faces of the students he had in his ESL classes in Chicago. "A human face," he writes,

> consists of other faces—the faces you inherited or picked up along
> the way, or the ones you simply made up—laid on top of each other
> in a messy superimposition .... I had students who would come to
> class with a different face every day.
>
> (105)

The struggle of Brik's immigrant students to refashion themselves was literally written on their faces in the superimposition of inherited, copied, and made up faces. This jumbled palimpsest of faces became their American face. To really know them, Brik had to discern what he calls "the deep faces beyond their acting out ... their new, American face" (106). This deep face is the one connected to their homeland. This becomes clear as Brik thinks about his strained relationship with his American wife, Mary, recalling that

> Mary could see no deep face of mine, because she did not know what
> my life in Bosnia had been like, what made me, what I had come
> from: she could see only my American face, acquired through failing
> to be the person I wanted to be.
>
> (106)

Taken together, these two passages sum up Brik's dilemma. In the first, both "meager Americanness" and Bosnian solidity are illusory, the one an acquired superficiality, the other a "costumed" fantasy, a "self-deception." In the second, the "deep" face seems associated with some kind of authentic self connected to a homeland, a self that exists beneath an "American face" that his students are "acting out." The problem is that the two passages cancel each other out. The depth privileged in the second passage and associated with "Bosnian" is cancelled out by the performed inauthenticity of being Bosnian in the first. It is not so much that there is no such thing as being Bosnian—or being American—but rather that both faces are acquired through a failure of being the actual person one wants to be, which in a sense is neither, but an amalgam of the two. Indeed, Brik is so worried about ever being able to be "American" that he resists the idea of having children with Mary because

> I was afraid they would become too American for me. I was afraid I would not understand them, I would hate what they became; they would live in the land of the free, and I would live in fear of being deserted.
>
> (254)

Brik's trip with Rora through Eastern Europe is ostensibly aimed at learning more about Averbuch and his family, but at the same time it is a kind of escape from the self he has fashioned in America and a journey back to his life in Bosnia (they end up in Sarajevo). As such, it enacts a kind of extinction. When they get to Kishinev (now called Chisinau) he and Rora visit the Jewish Community Center there, and later, a nearby cemetery, trying to learn something about the Averbuch family and their lives there. Finding himself suddenly alone there (Rora and their guide have wandered off), Brik has a moment in which his life in America simply falls away.

> Everything I had been was now very far away; I reached elsewhere. I could not remember how long ago I had left Chicago and Mary. I could not recall her face, what our house looked like, what it was that we called our life.
>
> (234)

The phrasing here is striking in its specificity. Not "I was else-where" but "I reached elsewhere," as if elsewhere were a place on the map where one could be. Memory becomes short-circuited, and then, Brik writes, "some part of my life ended there, among those empty graves; it was then that I started mourning. I can tell you that now, now that there is little but mourning" (235).

One of the ways in which Hemon weaves Brik's story together with Averbuch's is by laying their journeys across Eastern Europe over one another. Brik's trip with Rora to Chisinau (formerly Kishinev) and his eventual arrival in Sarajevo, where he was born, mirror in reverse Averbuch's journey with Isador from Kishinev to Chicago. These overlapping stories are full of border crossings, both literal and figural, and some of the most powerful passages in the novel evoke the border zones through which they pass. Passages like this give Brik a chance to emphasize Averbuch's status as a refugee, something that links the two of them. "Lazarus," Brik writes, "had spent time in Chernivtsi—Czernowitz it was back then—the first place he and I now shared, apart from Chicago," emphasizing that "no accounts of his life talk about his refugee years" (125). Czernowitz, he continues, "was his nowhere," a place where, in transit, he lived with other survivors of the pogrom in Kishinev. "Nowhere" is an uncanny kind of place name. To be nowhere is to be, well, nowhere, yet nowhere *is* someplace. To say your wallet is nowhere to be found does not mean it isn't someplace, and though the dictionary will tell us that nowhere refers to an unknown, distant, or obscure place (or state of being), it is still somewhere. Averbuch's nowhere is a place between, stateless, a border zone. It is at once the perfect metaphor for both Averbuch and Brik (indeed, Hemon's first novel in English, published in 2002, about a Bosnian refugee, was titled *Nowhere Man*) and a concrete place, characterized by what Brik calls a "border euphoria," the

> elation of nobody ever being at home; the freedom of no attachments possible; smugglers, the refugees, the gamblers, the conspirators, and the whores; the illegal crossings and the drunken fights at the beer hall—it was the Sodom of the empire .... Later, in Chicago, he and Isador remembered Czernowitz with some fondness and nostalgia; it was the last place where Lazarus was able to imagine the exciting details of a better future.
>
> (125)

This nowhere is as concrete as it could be, a place suspended and apart from the nation, with its borders, its restrictions, and its glib, imposed, sentimental fictions of identity, like the kitsch described in Brik's passage about the Bosnian Independence Day celebration. This nowhere is not so much a fantasy *place* as it is a place where fantasy is set free. Brik's description, quoted above, is "how I imagined it" (125), and in his imagination, Averbuch thinks of it as the last place where he could imagine a better future. In passages like this *The Lazarus Project* focuses, as both Tokarczuk's and Gordimer's novels do, on transit and flight. Though associated with possibility in *The Lazarus Project*, border zones remain a temporary point of passage, not an existential condition: "There was home and away-from-home in my life, and the space between the two was rife with borders. And if I violated the laws governing the home/away-from-home transitions, they would keep me away from home. It was that simple" (182). The difficulty of inhabiting a space between home and away-from-home is that the between space is itself "rife with borders."

FURTHER READING

Adichie, Chimamanda Ngozi. *The Thing Around Your Neck* (New York: Knopf, 2009).

Anzaldua, Gloria. *Borders/La Frontera* (San Francisco: Aunt Lute Books, 1987).

Lahiri, Jhumpa. *The Lowland* (New York: Knopf, 2013).

Ghosh, Amitav. *The Shadow Lines* (New York: Viking Penguin, 1989)

Scenters-Zapico, Natalie. *The Verging Cities: Poems* (Fort Collins: Colorado State University Press, 2015).

REFERENCES

Gordimer, Nadine. *The Pickup* (New York: Viking, 2001).

Hemon, Aleksandar. *The Lazarus Project* (New York: Riverhead, 2008).

Hemon, Aleksandar. *Nowhere Man: The Pronek Fantasies* (New York: Nan A. Talese, 2002).

Rios, Alberto. "Border: A Double Sonnet" in *A Small Story About the Sky* (Port Townsend: Copper Canyon Press, 2015).

MIGRATION

Home/away-from-home transitions are at the center of virtually all of the books we have discussed so far, from Tokarczuk's wide-ranging, at times elliptical, meditation on flight to Ghosh's focus on both migration and cultural identity in the Sundarbans, Cole's historical exploration of displacement and migration in ostensibly open cities like New York and Brussels, Sally Wen Mao's poems about the push–pull she experiences between the United States and China, and Gordimer's story about Julie and Ibrahim. It is important to note that while each of these books shares with *The Lazarus Project* an interest in the geopolitics of immigration, they operate as literary works in very different ways. Mao, of course, uses the resources of poetry rather than narrative fiction to explore many of the same issues covered by the novels we have been discussing. Among the novels, Ghosh's is arguably the most conventional. While the narrative perspective shifts regularly from Kanai, Piya, Fokir, and Nirmal, and while it occasionally shifts from the present to the past to fill in historical detail, the overall shape of the book is straightforward and sequential, moving temporally from Kanai and Piya's arrival to an eventual denouement and resolution. Cole's book, on the other hand, is dominated by a single narrative voice, Julius. Although the stories of other characters get told, they are almost always told by him, and it is his consciousness we inhabit. While his book, like Ghosh's, unfolds sequentially, that sequentiality is often disrupted by Julius' sometimes scholarly disquisitions on painting, music, architecture, and history, and by its changes in locality as it moves between New York, Lagos, and Brussels. The narrative structure of *The Pickup*, on the other hand, is highly schematic in a way that distinguishes it from each of the others. While it also unfolds in an unbroken temporal sequence, it is divided almost exactly in half, with the first part of the novel taking place in Johannesburg, and the second in Ibrahim's unnamed village, a shift that underscores the crucial relationship between place and identity, and serves to emphasize the different trajectories of the main characters. Where in *Open City* Julius' detachment, insularity, and propensity to over-intellectualize to a fault is enhanced by Cole's choice to have him control the narrative point of view, Gordimer, like Ghosh, chooses to continually shift her narrative point of view, from Julie to Ibrahim, but also from the two of them to other, more minor characters, like Julie's father.

Hemon's novel, by comparison, is rather strikingly unorthodox. While it has a kind of sequential structure organized around Brik's early interest in Averbuch and the story of his and Rora's travels in Eastern Europe, that sequentiality is radically disrupted by the narrative shifts back-and-forth in time between Averbuch's Chicago and Brik's, and between Brik and Rora's border crossings and Averbuch and Isador's. One way to think about the different narrative structures of these novels is to recall the distinction Tokarczuk makes in *Flight* between constellationality and sequencing. We will recall that in her novel we are told that the "foundational idea" of travel psychology is "constellationality," which is based on the conviction that "it is impossible to build a consistent cause-and-effect course of argument or a narrative with events that succeed each other casuistically and follow from each other" (77). Rather, Tokarczuk insists that "in order to reflect our experience more accurately, it would be necessary instead to assemble a whole, out of pieces of more or less the same size, placed concentrically on the same surface. Constellation, not sequencing, carries truth" (77). As we saw earlier, Tokarczuk's novel is itself organized as a constellation of stories with little in the way of sequencing to link them. Its truthfulness is tied less to what it says than to the form it employs. Of course, many of the individual stories that comprise *Flight* unfold sequentially, so the novel's form is characterized by an alternation between constellationality and sequence. Hemon's novel comes the closest in its narrative structure to Tokarczuk's because its sequential trajectory is constantly augmented by what Tokarczuk characterizes as constellationality.

Noting these different formal characteristics helps call attention to the aesthetic diversity we find in transnational writing that focuses on immigration, migration, and the plight of the refugee. This diversity is reflected in three recent novels about transnational immigration, Jenny Erpenbeck's *Go, Went, Gone* (2015), Mohsin Hamid's *Exit West* (2017), and Helon Habila's *Travelers* (2019). Erpenbeck's novel (translated into English by Susan Bernofsky), explores the unlikely relationship a newly retired professor named Richard develops with a group of refugees in contemporary Berlin. It has a conventional, sequential narrative structure, sticks to Richard's point of view, and is as much about the nature and development of his relationship with the refugees as it is about their plight. Although centered in Berlin, the stories it tells cut across Italy, the Mediterranean, and a wide range of African countries. Habila's novel, on the other hand, is organized around the perspective of a Nigerian immigrant living in the United States who has come to Berlin with his wife, a photographer named Gina who is using funds from a fellowship to produce a series of portraits of refugees she calls *Travelers*. Beginning with the narrator's curiosity about one of Gina's subjects, a refugee who calls himself Mark, Habila's novel expands to tell the stories of multiple refugees whose lives are intertwined. Although Habila employs a third-person narrative voice throughout, the novel is divided into six books, each of which tells its subject's story from their own point of view, as the novel moves from Berlin to Greece, Switzerland, Italy, Great Britain, and the United States. The structure of Habila's novel, then, has a kind of affinity with the constellational structure we find in *Flights*. Unfolding as a loosely connected but out-of-sequence set of portraits like those Gina is painting, *Travelers* gets at the collective truth of the stories it tells by ordering them concentrically, as a constellation of stories linked through juxtaposition rather than sequence.

Hamid's *Exit West*, on the other hand, much like Erpenbeck's novel, unfolds sequentially and is told from the point of view of an omniscient narrator. It follows the flight of a single young couple from an unnamed city being ripped apart by sectarian violence (probably Lahore, Pakistan, but its being unnamed drives home the point that it could be any number of cities around the world) as they become refugees in search of a new home. Where both

Erpenbeck and Habila narrate their novels in a traditionally realist mode, however, Hamid employs a device normally associated with magical realism: the couple slip in a moment from one place to another through magic portals, traveling first to Greece, then London, and finally to California. While both Erpenbeck and Habila—like Hemon—are committed to focusing on the arduous *journeys* their characters have made to flee oppression, violence, and economic inequality, Hamid skips narrating these journeys altogether by magically dropping his characters into each of the successive places they arrive. Both *Go, Went, Gone* and *Travelers* arrange the narrative points of view so that the plight of the refugees they are describing is being observed by someone else whose experience is also the subject of the novel, whereas the narrator of *Exit West* is anonymous and has no stake, as a character, in what happens to the two protagonists.

In what follows, our discussion of these novels emphasizes the very different narrative approaches these writers take in engaging with migration, displacement, and the plight of refugees. This discussion is followed by an analysis of Marwa Helal's genre-bending *Invasive Species*, a book that blends poetry, memoir, and journalism with quotation and pastiche from other works in an approach to writing about borders, mobility, and migration that reaches beyond the limits and possibilities of any single genre. In so doing, Helal has fashioned a book that explores the limits and possibilities of borders by transgressing them in the very form it takes.

GO, WENT, GONE, JENNY ERPENBECK (2015)

The heart of *Go, Went, Gone* is its exploration of the relationship Richard develops with the African refugees he befriends. This link is embodied in the narrative structure of the book as Richard's story unfolds as his relationship to the refugees deepens. As he gets to know them they tell him their stories, which are folded seamlessly into the novel as we follow Richard's growing interest in them. The first story is Awad's, whose mother died giving birth to him in Ghana, and whose father moved the family to Libya when he was seven. Later, his father is shot and killed in the uprising that led to the overthrow of the Gaddafi regime, and Awad was rounded up and put on a boat for Sicily, and then later, flew to Germany in search of work (56–64). Later we hear from Rashid, a Nigerian who has ended up in Germany after fleeing from the horrors of sectarian and religious violence there (86–99), first to Niger, and then Libya, where he met the same fate as Awad, rounded up during the uprising against Gaddafi, then shunted off to a boat which eventually breaks down and capsizes, drowning 550 of the 800 people on board (193). Like Awad, Rashid makes his way to Sicily and, eventually, to Germany.

Crucial to the novel is the fact that Richard is himself the child of refugees. His parents fled Silesia (now part of Poland) after the Second World War and settled in what became the German Democratic Republic, or East Germany. "In the tumult of their departure," Erpenbeck writes,

> he almost got separated from his mother; he would have been left behind outright if it hadn't been for a Russian soldier, who, amid the press of people on the station platform, handed him to his mother through the train's window over the heads of many other resettlers.
>
> (17)

The initial violence and disorientation of this resettlement is compounded decades later by the fall of the Berlin Wall, the collapse of the GDR, and the reunification of Germany, another rupture that leaves Richard displaced and estranged in his own adopted homeland. The first time he attempts to attend a meeting between the refugees and the Berliners interested in their plight, which takes place in the Kreuzberg district, he gets lost because "he still doesn't know his way around West Berlin" (25). At one point, he asks himself whether "the only freedom the fall of the Berlin wall brought him" was "the freedom to go places he's afraid of" (25). Over the course of the novel Erpenbeck connects the borders Richard has had to cross with those crossed by the refugees he befriends, stressing how part of the connection he feels with them stems from his own experiences of displacement.

However, if the empathy Richard feels for these men is connected in some kind of psychic way to his own history, if he feels a kind of connection between their experiences and his own, that empathy has its roots less in a purely emotional response to their plight than in research and historical understanding. He is a recently retired professor of Classical Languages and Literatures, a scholar trained in the value of research and careful historical analysis. He first becomes aware of the refugees when he walks by chance past a group of them gathered in front of the Berlin Town Hall. He has no idea who they are or what they are doing there. It is only later that night when he is home watching the news on television that he learns the men in front of the town hall were African refugees staging a hunger strike. Their desire, as one of the placards they carry states, is to *"become visible"* (18). Richard's response to their visibility is to wonder why he didn't notice the demonstration, and then, as he often does while eating dinner in front of a TV screen full of the day's horrors, to feel "ashamed" and a bit guilty for his insulated privilege (18).

This shame is not only about his privilege but his ignorance as well, his own lack of knowledge about how these men got to Berlin, and about the places they came from:

> He reads that off the coast of the Italian island of Lampedusa, sixty-four of three hundred twenty-nine refugees drowned when their boat capsized, including some from Ghana, Sierra Leone, and Niger. He reads that somewhere over Nigeria a man from Burkina Faso fell from a height of ten thousand feet after stowing away in an aircraft's landing gear .... Where exactly is Burkina Faso? ... What is the capital of Ghana? Of Sierra Leone? Or Niger? ... He gets up and takes out his atlas. The capital of Ghana is Accra, the capital of Sierra Leone is Freetown, the capital of Niger Niamey. Had he ever known the names of these cities?
>
> (23)

In the next few weeks he begins reading "several books on the subject of the refugees and drawing up a catalog of questions for the conversations he wants to have with them" (38). Over the course of his research he comes to recognize that the history of European colonialism has brought these men to Berlin, that the bureaucratic hurdles they face here are a kind of "geometry" linked to the administration of colonial domination, that "the moment they signed an *agreement*, it became necessary to administer them," and he has learned from his research on the historical consequences of colonialism that "the colonized are smothered in bureaucracy, which is a pretty clever way to keep them from taking political action" (49). He has learned, as well, that the borders between African nations were created by Europeans (the Tuareg refugees "say that in the 1960s the French, by dividing up the region they had traditionally inhabited into five different countries, cut their political body into pieces" [140]) and "the thought occurs to him that the borders drawn by Europeans may have no relevance at all for Africans" (51).

Although much of what he has read since retiring is about "things he's known most of his life" the "additional knowledge he's acquired" has made those things "come together in new, different ways" (142). Here he thinks back to what he knows of "the path the Berbers may have taken," from the Caucasus to Egypt, then Libya and what is now Niger (143), and it crystallizes into a larger realization about the ceaseless nature of human migration:

> This movement of people across the continents has already been going on for thousands of years, and never once has this movement halted. There were commerce, and wars, and expulsions; people often followed the animals they owned in search of water and food, they fled from droughts and plagues, went in search of gold, salt, or iron, or else their faith in their own god could be pursued only in the diaspora. There was ruin and then transformation and reconstruction. There were better roads and worse ones, but never did movement cease.
>
> (143)

Richard's research has a number of functions in Erpenbeck's novel. First of all, it provides the reader a historical context in which to think about the plight of the refugees in her novel—and by extension the plight of contemporary refugees everywhere. It especially gives the Western reader of her novel a foothold, a perspective through which, as an outsider, to think about the African refugees at the center of the book. By doing so, Erpenbeck emphasizes the importance of understanding how historical forces have shaped contemporary events, and, perhaps more importantly, the relationship between intellectual thinking and what we call empathy. Empathy for others, the book insists, is not simply the result of feelings, of reflexive emotional responses. Rather, it has to be grounded in an intellectual grasp of how social, cultural, economic, and political forces shape historical subjects.

Indeed, the key point that links both Richard and the African refugees in *Go, Went, Gone* is that they are *all* rendered *as* historical subjects. This is where the importance of her focus on Richard's background becomes crucial, his being the child of refugees himself, his having nearly been lost as a young child in the chaos of a border crossing, his having grown up in a divided country with a border wall running down the center of his city, Berlin, the administrative center of the Holocaust. It is not as if Richard's life has been anywhere near as difficult as those of the African refugees he comes to care for. The point is that he comes to recognize beneath the surface of his comfortable life fault lines in his own experience that help him form a historical understanding of their situation. Much of this understanding is shaped by the way he comes to think about borders and the transitions involved in crossing through them. Beyond his own experience with the borders of Eastern Europe, his new, historical understanding of how national borders in Africa were imposed on Africans by Europeans, and the arduous challenge of negotiating contemporary borders as a refugee from poverty, civil war, and religious oppression, is his realization that borders—and border conflicts—travel. "A border, Richard thinks, can suddenly become visible, it can suddenly appear where a border never used to be: battles fought in recent years on the borders of Libya, or of Morocco or Niger, are now taking place in the middle of Berlin-Spandau" (209), an idea we encountered earlier in *The Pickup*. Another example, of course, would be the border formed by the Berlin Wall, an objective embodiment of the Cold War struggle between the Soviet Union and the West.

Wrapped up with the book's meditation on borders is its interest in transitions. "A border," Richard realizes early in the book, "is a place where, at least in mathematics, signs often change their value" (35). "At the border between a person's life and the other life lived by that same person," a transition always takes place, and Richard's interest is in understanding "how one makes the transition from a full, readily comprehensible existence to the life of a refugee" (39). That transition, as one of the African refugees, Awad, explains, is the process of *becoming foreign*. To cross a border, as a migrant or refugee, is to become foreign ... you don't have a choice. You don't know where to go. You don't know anything. I can't see myself anymore, can't see the child I used to be. I don't have a picture of myself anymore .... Becoming foreign. To yourself and others ... that's what a transition looks like.

(63)

Erpenbeck's choice to narrate her novel from Richard's perspective doubles its thematic focus. If the stories of Awad, Rashid, Khalil, and the other refugees as they struggle to become visible, find work, and attain legal status in Germany had not been focalized through Richard, but rather from the point of view of an omniscient third-person narrator, the thematic scope of the novel would have been much narrower. As important as their story is, exploring along with it Richard's transition from an ignorant bystander to an informed and active advocate gives Erpenbeck the opportunity to explore the question of his link to, and responsibility for the refugees. *Go, Went, Gone*, in this way, is neither an African nor a European story, but a story about the transnational historical entanglement of the two continents. As Richard absorbs that history, the reader absorbs it as well, and by linking Richard's status as the son of refugees and a man who has experienced displacement and estrangement in the West to the experience of the refugees, Erpenbeck emphasizes the deep structure of links between them. To be sure, she runs a risk both in making Richard's story so prominent a part of the novel, and by seeming at times to equate his problems with theirs. After all, nothing Richard has experienced bears any resemblance to the suffering of the African refugees he befriends, and there are times when his story, and the novel's call to sympathize with him, run the risk of distracting us from their story. But the result of that risk is a novel that forces Richard to think about his own complicity in their plight, to consider the aspects of his own experience that make him feel linked to them, and perhaps, most importantly, his own recognition that he has a responsibility to do something to help them.

TRAVELERS, HELON HABILA (2019)

If *Go, Went, Gone* challenges our assumptions regarding what a "German" novel can be about, Helon Habila's *Travelers* does the same thing with regard to the "African" novel. Erpenbeck's is a German novel in the sense that its author is German, and the novel is centered on events that take place in Berlin. But it has a transnational scope, both in terms of how the stories of individual refugees it tells take us to the Global South (southern Italy, Sicily, Lampedusa, and various countries throughout Africa) and also with regard to the histories of migration, colonialism, decolonization, and contemporary immigration that Richard researches. Both Erpenbeck and Habila are writing at a time in which the conventional idea of national boundaries as a shaping force in fiction is giving way to a focus on intersectional boundaries made elastic by unprecedented forms of mobility. Indeed, Habila has said that he thinks of himself as part of a second generation of African writers freed from the artificial boundaries of the nation and able to write about Africans and their experiences everywhere. He notes that "the first generation" of African writers, beginning with Chinua Achebe, were

> obliged to write about colonialism and the fight for independence. That was the dominant issue of the day. They couldn't do otherwise. Almost as if the African writer has been held captive by the politics of the nation. Now we can write about anything we want to write about.
> (interview with Tope Folarin, August 25, 2019, https://www.youtube.com/watch?v=qVLwYzaLofE)

He goes on to identify himself as belonging to a "post-national generation" of African writers, a generation that is "moving beyond the issue of the nation." In both novels, the boundaries between Germany and Africa dissolve into a transnational matrix of intersecting locations. In each of them, histories, cultural habits, and personal experiences both overlap and put pressure on conventional nation-state borders.

This is true for the African refugees in both novels, of course, but also for Richard and the unnamed narrator of *Travelers*. At the outset of Erpenbeck's novel, as we have seen, the borders for Richard between Germany and Africa are, paradoxically, both absolute and unknown. Over the course of the novel, not only do those borders become real to him, their histories also challenge his unconscious assumption that they are fixed, absolute, and somehow natural. He learns otherwise, that the borders between

African nations were inextricably bound up with Europe because they were drawn *up* by Europeans. But, perhaps more importantly, he also realizes that the borders that define Germany itself are not impermeable but porous. The very idea of the nation in *Go, Went, Gone* is put in question as "Africa" and "Germany" become redefined by their entanglement with one another. And of course, as he experiences the scrambling of these borders, Richard becomes redefined, increasingly foreign to himself. This, as we shall see, is what happens to the narrator of *Travelers* as well, for as he becomes immersed in the lives of the African migrants and refugees he meets in Berlin, his understanding of the nature of the borders that divide Germany from the countries of Africa becomes transformed, but more importantly, his own identity is increasingly redefined as well.

There is one more link between these novels that is important to stress, and that is the sense of urgency that produced them, and the transformative effect they had on their authors. In this respect the two books have much in common. Not only are they about the same migrant crisis in Germany, but the narrators of each novel are fictionalized versions of the authors themselves, and the stories they tell are fictionalized versions as well of those they collected from the migrants and refugees they befriended. Richard's experience in *Go, Went, Gone* is based on Erpenbeck's own involvement with the African refugees she writes about. Like Richard, she first heard about them from protests and newspaper articles, began to research the history behind their arrival, befriended them, conducted interviews with them, and, along with her friends, assisted them. She was at the time at work on another novel, but set it aside in order to write this book because she had a sense of urgency about the project. Habila's novel was the product of a similar experience. Like his narrator, a Nigerian living and teaching in America, Habila happened to be in Berlin on a fellowship in 2013 when he was asked by a magazine to write an article about the capsizing of one of the refugee boats that left over 300 people drowned. Researching the article, he developed a relationship with a number of the refugees, whom he subsequently interviewed. Their stories, interwoven with his own in the guise of the narrator, became the basis for his novel.

Notwithstanding these similarities, there are important differences between the two books, however. Some are purely literary, having to do with choices each author made about how to organize their novels and the narrative point of view from which they are told. Erpenbeck's novel, for example, unfolds in chronological order and, while it is narrated in the third person, the narrator's perspective is Richard's—an older, white German professor with a rambling home on a lake. Habila's novel, on the other hand, switches back and forth between first-person sections in which the narrator, a Nigerian teacher who lives in America, tells his own story, and his third-person rendering of the stories of six different refugees he has met, stories that unfold from their perspectives, not from the first-person narrator's. Moreover, rather than unfolding in chronological order, Habila's novel moves back-and-forth in time. While Erpenbeck's novel keeps the reader steadily focused on Richard's experience, broken up by relatively short glimpses of the refugees' own stories, *Travelers* devotes four and a half of its six chapters to refugee stories, with a particular stress on the circumstances surrounding their having to flee from home and the arduous nature of the journeys that have brought them to Germany (a significant departure from Hamid's decision to forego altogether the treatment of his characters' journeys from one country to another).

Unlike Erpenbeck's narrator, Habila's tells his own story in the first person in Books 4 and 6, and a good part of Book 5 (the novel is divided into six books). While Richard is implicitly part of the story in *Go, Went, Gone*, the narrator of *Travelers* is a key character, and he tells the story of his personal life back in the United States, and his involvement with the refugees he meets directly to the reader. For this reason, and because he is himself a Nigerian immigrant, the distance between them is much less than that between Richard and the men he meets. More importantly, at a point late in the novel, the narrator mistakenly leaves a train with the bag of an African man who is in the country illegally and, when he arrives in Italy he is sent to a series of refugee camps in Lampedusa, Greece, and Sicily before being deported to Tunisia. He thus falls into the very experience he has been describing in the stories about the refugees he has met. He is finally able to make his way to London and to reclaim his identity, but, in a highly symbolic move, Habila has him return to Africa with one of the women he met in Berlin.

While both of these novels deal with the material, logistical, and legal challenges of migration as a refugee, they also explore the inner lives of their characters. One example is their treatment of memory. Both deal poignantly with the paradoxical relationship between migration and memory, for while memories are the only link to home and family they are also a reminder of loss and the emptiness of the future. In *Go, Went, Gone*, for example, Richard recalls how one of the refugees, Rashid, told him that

> not even his memories of his wonderful life with his family could console him, since these memories are bound up with the pain of his loss and that's all there was. Rashid said he wished he could cut off his memory. Cut it away.
>
> (277)

In response, Richard thinks to himself of the pain that comes with "a life in which an empty present is occupied by a memory that one cannot endure, in which the future refuses to show itself" (277). Habila also stresses how memory can keep the past alive, even if—or when—it's been erased, but yet also feed a false reality. One of the refugees in *Travelers*, Manu, makes a point to visit Checkpoint Charlie in Berlin every Sunday at an appointed time because he made a pact with his wife that, if they became separated, they would meet there (he with their daughter, Rachida, and her with their son). While it seems likely to the reader that his wife and son have drowned, he visits every week. At one point, he is confronted by another refugee, Hannah, about the seeming futility of all this.

> Maybe it is time to let go, Manu ... Rachida ... She knows her mother is never coming. She is doing this just to please you .... Listen ... my husband ... [ellipses in original] he is not coming either. He died, killed in front of my eyes.
>
> (97)

Hannah's surmise is that Manu knows they are dead, blames himself, and so goes to Checkpoint Charlie every Sunday as a kind of penance. "He won't give up," she tells the narrator, "he will go to Checkpoint Charlie every Sunday. Rachida will come with him. They will walk past the souvenir shops and ice cream stalls, together. If they keep their memories alive, then nothing has to die" (97).

INVASIVE SPECIES, MARWA HELAL (2019)

While each of the writers we have been discussing so far links the history of migration and mobility to the lives of their contemporary characters, they also use the form of the novel to dramatize how identity, shaped by transnational forces, is not simply an interior state but something materially defined by geography, language, and nationality. They use the resources of narrative fiction to stress how national belonging is given form by race, ethnicity, language, the law, and bureaucracy (prominent in *The Pickup*, but see also *The Queue*, 2016, by Basma Abdel Aziz). Marwa Helal's *Invasive Species* explores these topics as well, but it breaks altogether with the conventions of literary genre, unfolding before the reader as a kind of twenty-first-century mash-up of poetry, fiction, and journalism, all of which are supplemented by the incorporation of dictionary and encyclopedia entries quoted verbatim—and by an unorthodox graphic layout—that together turn the book into a kind of hybrid literary form. Ultimately, *Invasive Species* is a book about the impact of difference and diversity on things we often want to think of as pure and clearly defined, and so the form of the book is an experiment in its own proposal, that systems—biological, human, and literary—always benefit from diversity and the transgression of borders. *Invasive Species* is, relative to conventional literary genres, an invasive species. Transgressing the boundaries between poetry, fiction, and non-fiction, Helal's book opens up the possibilities of how literature can approach transnational experience (her book centers on the United States, Egypt, and the Middle East), and it does so by embedding the very disruptions of that experience in its own form. In so doing, it moves fluidly between the loosely realist mode employed in their novels by Habila and Erpenbeck, and the magical realism of Hamid's *Exit West*.

While distinguished by the fluidity of its literary modes, *Invasive Species* is, fundamentally, a kind of memoir or autobiography. It tells the story of Helal's own Kafkaesque experience trying to get back to the United States, where she grew up, after having been sent back to Egypt, where she was born, because delays in processing her application for permanent residency in the United States by the I.N.S led to her deportation, since she had legally "aged out" (34) of eligibility for permanent residency. While much of the book is taken up with her efforts in Egypt to straighten out the bureaucratic tangle so that she may return home to the United States, the initial section of the book, "Invasive Species," is composed of poems. It is not until Section II, "Immigration as a Second Language," that the reader gets Helal's backstory. Here, the book abruptly shifts from poetry to prose, moving into a narrative and journalistic mode. By the final Section III, "i am made to leave I am made to return," the borders between prose and poetry, between imagination and reporting, already blurred in the first two sections, collapse altogether, as it moves back-and-forth seamlessly between them.

Since in all three sections of the book language, and the way in which it shapes identity, reality, and belonging, is a central topic, it makes sense that the poems comprising Section I explore this topic in a range of ways. Its epigram, from Chinua Achebe, points the way: "Let no one be fooled by the fact that we may write in English, for we intend to do unheard of things with it." The Achebe quote reminds us that Helal could have written the book in either English or Arabic, a reminder reinforced by the reference to Arabic in the first poem in this section, entitled "poem to be read from right to left." This poem, which does literally (like Arabic) have to be read from right to left to make sense, deals with how she learned her first language second, but was treated as a "native" speaker everywhere she went, and it serves to introduce the recurring idea that language inevitably helps define identity. Later, in a poem entitled "poem for the beings who arrived," language in general and poetry in particular is described as a mode of conversing with "broken wings" (evoked in a modified quote from Pablo Neruda): "if you ask me where i come from, I have/to converse with broken things" (10). Broken wings and broken things reference language, but they get associated later with the "broken beings" of the title: "we are the broken beings who/ arrived with glass for hearts, poetry is instrument; allows us to see through thought" (10). To speak of identity from Helal's perspective, that is to say from the perspective of the displaced and marginalized, and in another language, is to use a broken thing.

This poem introduces the idea that different languages—poetic, fictional, journalistic—reflect on and refract reality in very different ways, each of which has its own value. Poetry is her "instrument" here because poetry "allows us to see through thought," which is to say it explores migrancy, mobility, and flight from a perspective beyond thought, beyond what can be captured by the journalistic prose that will dominate the next section. A later poem, "freewrite for an audience" follows up on and reiterates this distinction. Writers "like us" (she has just referenced Julio Cortázar and Roberto Bolaño), "we have/no plot," and the poems here are to be considered as "my archive" (12): "the future needs women's archives more than anything else, when/they cull us, they will see it was never a man's world at all" (13). A later poem, "invasive species self-questionnaire," links code-switching to Du Bois' well-known concept of "double consciousness," to "inner conflict," and to "what happens when the colonizer's blood runs through yours" (15). Poetry, Helal is insisting here, has value precisely because it operates beyond "thought" and "plot," and is open to the kind of productive, imaginative insights produced by code switching.

One of the key links emphasized throughout the poems in this opening section is the one between "home and/language and how in some ways they have come to mean the same/thing" (22). Helal's use of the Achebe quote in her epigram to this section, followed by the initial poem that has, like Arabic, to be read left to right, foregrounds her two languages and how they represent or embody two overlapping, simultaneously lived identities. Home is a language, and language is a home. Both are central to her identity, hence the invocation of Du Bois' concept of "double consciousness." Helal uses the final poems in this section to set up a contrast with the more self-consciously journalistic section that follows. "Dreamwork," for example, begins "poems do work journalism cant and dreams do work only dreams/do" (25). This line gestures back to the fact that poems do not have plots, that this section is an archive of the imagination. If home is a kind of language, so too is immigration, and so Section II is given the title "Immigration as a Second Language." It is not until this section, a mix of narrative, memoir, journalism, historiography, and political writing, that we get Helal's story, her birth in Egypt, her arrival at age two and a half in the United States, her parents' decision to stay in America, and later, her receipt of a deportation notice.

Much of the rest of this section is taken up with the byzantine bureaucratic hurdles she encounters in repeated visits to the U.S. embassy in Cairo (44–53), where, despite submitting "paperwork that proves our stay in the U.S was legal" (49) she is repeatedly denied a visa. At one point, she is told by an agent, "I'll refuse you for the fun of it" (49). It is not until 2013 that she is sworn in as a U.S. citizen. In this section Helal foregrounds the troubling vocabulary that surrounds and polices immigration in sections that focus on terms like "alien" (36) and "asylum," rendered in the form of a page-long dictionary entry. It becomes increasingly grim, beginning with "political asylum" and "protection" and running to "committed to an asylum," "lunatic asylum," and "confined to an asylum" (37). The terms "Birthplace" (38), "Census" (39), "Deportation" (43), and "Naturalization" (59) are also invoked. In each of these entries Helal explores the origin and multiple meanings of each term, teasing out the insidious side of each.

The term "naturalization" is particularly important to her use throughout the book of the title's key trope, invasive species. "Naturalize," she notes, is both a legal and a biological term. It means "to confer upon (an alien) the right and privileges of a citizen," but also "to introduce (organisms into a region and cause them to flourish as if native)" (59). Later in the book she explains that her use of "invasive species" is an attempt to use irony to counter the negative force of these terms:

> Homeland security's terms: "legal" or "illegal." Both end up with many of the same consequences: soul loss, loss of familial ties, and in some cases, loss of native culture and language. Both terms inherently deny the immigrant's humanity.
> So I made my own term: I, Invasive species.

(88)

"Invasive" here conjures up the pervasive fear of immigration as a form of alien invasion, and "species" references how those fears are linked to concepts of racial and ethnic purity. Helal's "invasive species" trope, then, is aimed at blunting those fears by linking invasive species to thoroughly natural biological processes. For example, on p. 82 her book reproduces a photocopy of an abstract from a report in the "Illinois Natural History Survey and Progress in Ecology" entitled "Native fish diversity alters the effect of an invasive species on food webs" (by Michael P. Carey and David H. Wahl), which stresses the value of the biodiversity introduced by invasive species. A report on how "aquatic communities have been altered by invasive species," it concludes that

> overall, the invader reduced resources for native species, and the effect scaled with how the invader was incorporated into the community. Higher native diversity mitigated the impact of the invader, confirming the need to consider biodiversity when predicting the impacts of invasive species.
>
> (82)

While Helal mostly leaves it to the reader to understand the implications here for seeing the value of diversity within human communities, she does tie together a little later the link between the science of biodiversity and how cultural systems operate, noting that the "America I return to is part of a world that is becoming more aware of how we are inextricably connected. We are each other and complicit in these systems .... In this sense, the world is one country" (91). Here, we ought to note, Helal echoes Zadie Smith's extensive exploration of biological and cultural diversity in her transnational novel set in multicultural London, *White Teeth* (2000).

Helal's play on words throughout the book with regard to the vocabulary surrounding identity, immigration, and national belonging highlights the value of poetic language in exploring political, cultural, and psychological issues. However, as we noted earlier, the book moves fluidly between the idioms of the poetic, the autobiographical, and the journalistic. While much of the book is either composed of poems or written in poetic language, significant portions, as we have seen, also include reports, dictionary entries, quotations, abstracts, and long sections that interweave journalism and poetry. There is reporting in the poetry, and poetry in the reporting (in Cairo, Helal worked for a time as a journalist for *Egypt Today* [83]). Having told a customs agent at Heathrow Airport that she is a writer, the agent asks what kind of writing she does. "i tell him I used to be a journalist but now im a poet" (97), but in fact the two discourses flow together in her book, each an invasive species relative to the other which, together, foster the book's generic diversity. In the final analysis, she writes (in a short poem entitled "generation of feeling"), "i am trying to tell you something about how/rearranging words/rearranges the universe" (98).

The universe Helal is particularly interested in is the one dubbed by the West "the Middle East." Throughout the book she stresses the constructed, artificial nature of this transnational space, and the geopolitical forces that have shaped it. Early in the book we encounter a poem entitled "the middle east is missing" (18–20). The Middle East is "missing" for Helal in the sense that it represents an absence, a conflation of unrelated entities, cultures, and people:

> wha do osama bin laden and I have in common? saddam?
> qadaffi? mubarak? sharon?
> peres? is kashmir? is asia? is persia? is europe? is iran? is jordan? is
> kurd? a language? a
> religion? cuisine? borders on bordering? what do you and I have in
> common? red sea dead sea an empire syria iraq say kurd
> say we were occupied
> a people under siege of make xenophobia believe ...

Much of this stems, of course, from Helal's own association with "the Middle East," the assumption that this is where she is from even though she was raised in the United States. But what does she have in common with the disparate figures she mentions, and what do they have in common with each other? And, what is "the Middle East," anyway? A language? A religion? A cuisine? To what extent, she asks, is it a product of Western xenophobia? "Say we were occupied" is crucial here, but then the poem immediately veers in another direction: "say we did it to ourselves./say: complicit" (18). But then this: "maybe it is a cry for help. maybe it is just a cry. say palestinian" (19).

These multiple angles on the "Middle East" stress its historically constructed nature, its status as the product of geopolitical forces. Helal follows up on this poem much later in the book with another

entitled "the middle east[1] is not only missing/it has a serious problem" (109). Here, she insists that if you "buy into" the "ideology"
behind constructions like "the Middle East" you are buying into
"white ideology and its byproduct: all oppressive systems" (109). The
"Middle East" is missing for Helal in the sense that it does not exist
other than as a discursive and political product of the West. The
footnote after "east" in the poem's title takes the reader to a page-
long discussion of the origins of the term in the form of a quotation
from the online *Encyclopedia Britannica*. It constitutes a brief history
lesson on how "modern Western geographers and historians tended
to divide what they called the Orient into three regions," the Near
East, the Middle East, and the Far East (110). In stressing the Western
geopolitical forces that shaped the Middle East, and insisting on the
term's "complicity in oppressing black and/palestinian people," Helal
challenges the reader's assumption that the Middle East (which of
course includes her birthplace, Egypt) is an actual place, and instead
insists on its status as a discursive and geopolitical construction that
elides the diversity it actually contains.

One of the central questions implicit in Helal's treatment of the
"Middle East" has to do with its very nature. Is there, in fact, such
a thing as the "Middle East," and if so, how do we identify its
authenticity? Is it an actual place? Is its authenticity a function of
that place, that is, rooted in the land, the soil, the geography? Is it
grounded in language? Or is it cultural, marked by things like its
cuisine and the way people dress? Is Helal's book an American or
an Egyptian one? Does its having been written in English make it
Western? If it was written in Arabic, would it be a Middle Eastern
text? If it is Western, does that make its observations about Egypt
and the "Middle East" inauthentic? And, conversely, does its
grounding in Egyptian and "Arabic" culture make its observations
about America somehow inauthentic?

Many of these questions are confronted early in the book in a
poem entitled "poem for brad who wants me to write/about the
pyramids[1]." According to the poem, "Brad" thinks that in Helal's
poems about Egypt "the substance is lacking a center," and a
"traditional plot" (7). Brad "says/egypt is a wonderfully exciting
place" but that her poems have "scenes of policemen" where they
should be about the "the pyramids." He wants "to see more egypt
in my writing." Halal links Brad's protestations about the discursive

element in her poems about Egypt to the "poets" who insist about poetry "show, don't tell," because he would prefer cliché images to critical discussion. "What brad means," the poet tells us, is that "he/wants to see camels and more of his own/ideas of egypt in my work." Helal here calls our attention to Brad's desire for a faux authenticity in her poems about Egypt. The link between Brad's desire and a faux authenticity is elaborated in the footnote at the end of the title of the poem. It consists of a long quote from *The Argentine Writer and Tradition* (1961) by Jorge Luis Borges. Borges argues that "what is truly native can and often does dispense with local color" (8). His example? "In the Koran there are no camels." As an Arab, Borges points out, Mohammed "had no reason to know that camels were especially Arabian; for him they were a part of reality," whereas, "the first thing a falsifier, a tourist, an Arab nationalist would do is have a surfeit of camels, caravans of camels, on every page." Helal's point in quoting Borges is not so much that authenticity has no value, but that authenticity often translates into a series of clichés rooted, when it comes to the Middle East, in what the critic Edward Said called Orientalism. To the extent authenticity ought to correspond to the reality of a place, the reality of Egypt, for Helal, has less to do with camels and pyramids than it does with the omnipresence of police in the street and the cruelty of America's embassy there.

FURTHER READING

Abulhawa, Susan. *Mornings in Jenin* (New York: Bloomsbury, 2010).

Castillo, Elaine. *America Is Not the Heart* (New York: Viking, 2019).

Hamid, Mohsin. *Exit West* (New York: Riverhead, 2017).

Otsuka, Julia. *The Buddha in the Attic* (New York: Knopf, 2011).

Thein, Madeline. *Do Not Say We Have Nothing* (New York: W.W. Norton, 2016).

Vecchione, Patrice and Alyssa Raymond, eds, *Ink Knows No Borders: Poems of the Immigrant and Refugee Experience* (New York: Seven Stories Press, 2019).

REFERENCES

Aziz, Basma Abdel. *The Queue* (London: Melville House, 2016).

Erpenbeck, Jenny. *Go, Gone, Went* (New York: New Directions, 2017).

Hamid, Mohsin. *Exit West* (New York: Riverhead, 2017).

Helal, Marwa. *Invasive Species* (Brooklyn: Nightboat Books, 2019).

Helon, Habila. *Travelers* (New York: W.W. Norton and Company, 2019).

Smith, Zadie. *White Teeth* (New York: Random House, 2000).

IDENTITY

This chapter follows up on the questions about authenticity Helal discusses in *Invasive Species*, exploring how they are taken up by a range of transnational literary works that are particularly interested in identity, a topic treated by virtually all of the texts we have been discussing, each of which involves characters whose familial, social, and cultural moorings have become upended, and who find themselves having to adapt in multiple ways to new locations, traditions, and expectations. Identity, of course, is defined by a constellation of forces—most prominently place, nation, history, race, and culture—but it is complicated as well by notions of authenticity and belonging that, while they are meant to define inherent qualities, often tend to essentialize and exclude those marked as Other. For this reason, authenticity is a fraught term in discussions of identity in transnational literature. Is there really such a thing as authenticity, and if so, where do we find it? To what extent ought the project of transnational literature be dedicated to representing the authenticity of things like identity and culture? Who has the authority to call something authentic? Does one have to be a member of a particular culture to recognize what is authentic about it? Can outsiders really grasp what is authentic about a place or people? All of these questions, of course, are made complex by the historical weight of colonial domination, and they become politically and culturally complicated during decolonization. Colonialism systematically seeks to obliterate indigenous cultures and their practices. We can think of those cultures as having been authentic, but to what degree is that authenticity recoverable with the end of colonization, and is such a recovery even desirable in a postmodern age dominated by cultural and economic globalization? While this is a particular problem in postcolonial nations, to what extent are formerly colonized countries ever really "post" colonial? Critics are divided on this question, with many insisting that the "post" in postcolonial is misleading, since it is questionable whether any country that has been systematically colonized is ever able to recover its authentic indigenous identity.

It makes more sense to see authenticity not as an actual or empirical thing that one can identify and recover, but rather, as a term that is used strategically to categorize people, cuisine, music, and literature in ways that often have behind them some kind of political or ideological agenda. The Nigerian writer, Chimamanda Ngozi Adichie makes this point eloquently in her TED Talk discussed earlier, "The Danger of a Single Story" (2009). The danger of single stories, for Adichie, is precisely that they are often based on faux authenticity, a set of clichéd assumptions about others that are told so often that they are taken for reality. In Helal's *Invasive Species*, Brad's fixation on camels and pyramids, his assumption that they embody something authentic about Egypt, is an example. Adichie approaches the question of authenticity by telling the story of "a professor who once told me that my novel was not authentically African." She acknowledges that the novel had many failings, but adds, "I had not quite imagined that it had failed to achieve something called African authenticity. In fact, I did not know what African authenticity was." "My professor told me that my characters were too much like him, an educated and middle class man. My characters drove cars. They were not starving. Therefore, they were not authentically African." Adichie makes two important points here. First, authenticity is in the eye of the beholder. It can lead to cliché and the invocation of damaging stereotypes. Second, authenticity is not something that is objective and empirical. It is a social and historical construct, which is why Adichie can say that she did not even know what African authenticity was. She follows her comments about authenticity with the insistence that it is "impossible to talk about the single story without talking about power." Stories, she stresses, are defined by power: "how they are told, who tells them, when they are told, how many stories are told, are really dependent on power." "Power is the ability not just to tell the story of another person, but to make it the definitive story of that person." From this point of view Brad's protestations about Helal's Egypt poems are not simply aesthetic. They are an exercise of rhetorical power that ultimately have a political dimension.

"JUMPING MONKEY HILL," CHIMAMANDA NGOZI ADICHIE (2009)

Adichie explores the general question of authenticity in literature in one of the stories in her collection, *The Thing Around Your Neck*. In "Jumping Monkey Hill," a Nigerian writer named Ujunwa is one among a number of writers attending an African Writer's Workshop outside of Cape Town, South Africa, run by a white British academic named Edward Campbell. The main focus of the story is on the relationship between Campbell's sexual objectification of Ujunwa and the story she is writing at the workshop about a woman named Chioma who is being sexually harassed as she explores the possibility of employment with a bank. Adichie's story carefully weaves together Campbell's treatment of Ujunwa with the harassment Chioma is experiencing. The question of what constitutes authentic African writing begins to surface when the attendees read portions of their story at the workshop. The first story the attendees discuss is by a Zimbabwean writer and concerns a secondary schoolteacher who is told by his Pentecostal minister that witches have tied up his wife's womb and they will not be able to have a child until the witches confess. Ujunwa and others praise the story, but Campbell insists the story is "pasé ... when one considered all the other things happening in Zimbabwe under the horrible" dictator, Robert Mugabe (107). The next story read is by a Senegalese writer we have earlier learned is lesbian, and it is dismissed by Campbell because "homosexual stories of this sort weren't reflective of Africa, really" (108). Both stories are rejected by Campbell, who is white, because they do not fit his own notion of African authenticity.

It is at this point in the story that Ujunwa pushes back, asking "which Africa?" Campbell responds that he is "keen on the real Africa and not the imposing of Western ideas on African venues" (108). "How African is it," he asks, "for a person to tell her family that she is homosexual?", to which the Senegalese writer responds,

"I am Senegalese!" Stories about the "real" or authentic Africa, in Campbell's view, are not about witchcraft or homosexuality but the politics of Mugabe's dictatorship. This view of authentic African writing is reinforced later in the evening when a Tanzanian writer reads "an excerpt of his story about the killings in the Congo, from the point of view of a militiaman," who is "full of prurient violence" (109). Although Ujunwa feels it "read like a piece from *The Economist* with cartoon characters painted in," Campbell has given it pride of place as the lead story in his journal, *Oratory*. Things come to a head the evening Ujunwa reads an excerpt from her story about the sexual harassment her character, Chioma, had to struggle with. When she finishes, a writer from Uganda praises the story for being "strong" and "believable," and compliments her for "capturing Lagos well" (113). This praise is followed by more from a South African writer who found it a "realistic portrayal of what women were going through in Nigeria" (113). Campbell, however, insists that "it is never quite like that in real life, is it," calling the reader's attention to his blindness in treating Ujunwa in the same way her character is treated. "The whole thing is implausible" (114), he defensively insists. "This is agenda writing, it isn't a real story of real people" (114). The scene ends with Ujunwa revealing that the story was her own, that she was Chioma. It *was* the real story of a real person.

For Campbell, "real" or authentic African writing is about men, politics, and military action, and so the stories by women writers in the workshop, since they focus on the reality of their own experiences, are dismissed as inauthentic. Campbell's dismissal of the women's stories as "agenda writing" is particularly telling, since it calls attention to the fact there is an agenda implicit in his own argument about what is authentic about Africa, which in turn underscores the fact that assertions about what is authentic about a culture often have an agenda and are linked to the exercise of power Adichie speaks of in her TED Talk. As both Helal and Adichie make clear, the question of authenticity, posed within the larger context of the history of colonialism and decolonization, is always a vexed one, and nowhere more so than in transnational literature. The issues here, of course, overlap with those we discussed earlier with regard to Kwame Appiah's argument about culture and contamination. As we will recall, Appiah argues there is no such thing as cultural purity, which, like authenticity, is a kind of illusion because cultures are not fixed and static but constantly changing through contact and exchange with other cultures. This is especially the case in the late twentieth and early twenty-first centuries, of course, a time in which cultural and economic globalization have transformed cultures all around the world. This is why Adichie can say that she really had no idea what African authenticity was. What is "real" about personal and cultural behavior is in a constant state of flux and change, and assertions regarding authenticity—and complaints about inauthenticity—have to be understood in the context of the exercise of the kind of power Adichie discusses.

"THE SONG OF LAWINO," OKOT P'BITEK (1966)

Literary treatments of authenticity and identity explored in the context of colonization and decolonization in Africa have been deeply influenced by "The Song of Lawino," published in 1966 by the Ugandan poet, Okot p'Bitek. First published in his native language, Acoli Luo, it was later translated into English and had enormous influence among successive generations of writers in Africa and beyond. "The Song of Lawino" is quintessentially a postcolonial poem. As such, it deals with the impact of cultural colonization on identity in ways that are broadly applicable. Published four years after Uganda achieved its independence from Britain, the poem struggles with the question of how to reconcile Uganda's traditional Acoli culture with Western influence, and hence, with individual identity. It is important to note that p'Bitek himself was both schooled in modernist poetry *and* dedicated to recovering traditional African oral poetry, so in his poetic practice he lived the challenge of negotiating tradition and modernity. He was also deeply influenced by the Harlem Renaissance, the Negritude movement, the Black Consciousness Movement, and the Black Aesthetics Movement. Lawino, the poem's speaker, is a woman fiercely dedicated to traditional Acoli cultural practices and beliefs. She is married to Ocol, who has become deeply Westernized and taken a lover, Clementine, who shares his affinity for Western culture. From Lawino's point of view, her pretensions to whiteness are as offensive as her having taken up with her husband. While the poem, akin to the Western form of the dramatic monologue, is animated by Lawino's resentment toward her husband's lover, this resentment becomes the context for an expansive critique of Westernization and the damage Lawino observes it doing to traditional culture (for a contemporary treatment of these issues in a South African context, see Zakes Mda's 2000 novel, *The Heart of Redness*).

The poem, organized into 13 sections that cover in a systematic way a range of cultural topics, contains a litany of complaints that foreground Ocol's adoption of Western culture and the oppressive shadow it casts over his marriage to Lawino. Among other things, he resents her blackness, the fact she cannot read English, that she does not like Western music, and has not converted to Christianity. All of this gets introduced in the opening lines of the poem: "He abuses me in English ... He says I am primitive/Because I cannot play the guitar,/He says my eyes are dead/And I cannot read,/He says my ears are blocked/And cannot hear a single foreign/word" (35). "My husband pours scorn/On Black People," and "He says we are all Kaffirs./We do not know the ways of /God/We sit in deep darkness/And do not know the Gospel ... And that we are all sorcerers" (35). Lawino's disdain for her husband's lover, moreover, stems in part from her use of white powder to lighten her skin ("The beautiful one aspires/To look like a white woman ... Tina dusts powder on her face/And it looks so pale" [37]), and because "She says she fears getting fat ... She says a beautiful woman/Must be slim like a white/Woman" (40).

While Lawino is upset by her husband's infidelity, what outrages her even more is his adopting of white culture and his demonizing of traditional Acoli culture. Lawino is adamant that "I do not understand/The ways of foreigners/But I do not despise their customs" the way her husband does (41). The third section of the poem, "I Do Not Know the Dances of White People," covers a range of complaints about cultural matters, the fact that Ocol criticizes her for not learning Western dances ("My husband laughs at me/Because I cannot dance white/men's dances;/He despises Acoli dances" [47]), that she does not "smoke cigarettes/Like white women," while men like him "dress up like white/men,/As if they are in the white/man's country" (45). Similarly, section five, "The Graceful Giraffe/Cannot Become a Monkey" criticizes her husband for adopting Western dress and speaks of the beauty of traditional Acoli hairstyles and modes of dress. Section six, "The Mother Stone/Has a Hollow Stomach," deals with her husband's disdain for traditional Acoli cuisine, while section eight, "I Am Ignorant of the/Good Word in the Clean Book" criticizes not just Ocol's adoption of Christianity but his disdain for, and internalized phobia of, traditional Acoli spiritual beliefs and practices. "He says/ He has left behind/All sinful things/And all superstitions and fears/ He says/He has no wish/To be associated any more/With the devil" (82). Throughout the poem she criticizes her husband not just for adopting Western culture, but for disrespecting the traditions of his own culture:

> Like beggars
> You take up white men's
> adornments,
> Like slaves or war captives
> You take up white men's ways.
> Didn't the Acoli have
> adornments?
> Didn't Black People have their
> ways?
>
> (49)

"Song of Lawino" registers, at the very moment decolonization in Africa gets under way, deep contradictions that raise the question of whether there is even such a thing as a *post*colonial period. How can Lawino's Uganda be *post*colonial if the very culture of the colonizer has been internalized by so many people like Ocol, and if Lawino's embrace of traditional Acoli culture is seen as primitive and backward by fellow Ugandans eager to embrace cultural modernity and economic modernization? The larger questions p'Bitek explores here call attention to the role that notions of authenticity and cultural identity play in the political process associated with independence and economic development (issues explored at length in Mda's novel as well). Ocol's embrace of modernity, a version of cosmopolitanism, seems aligned with a vision of economic and political modernization that constitutes "progress," while in his view Lawino's embrace of traditional Acoli cultural beliefs and practices, viewed by him as primitive, superstitious, and backward, is a drag on that progress. At the heart of the poem is not so much the force of Lawino's critique of this modernization, or Ocol's demonizing of traditional Acoli culture, but the question of how to reconcile their two views. To what extent should Acoli authenticity and identity be measured using Lawino's long list of traditional beliefs, values, and practices? Or, is authenticity a kind of fabrication that, to the extent it is embraced, may hold the newly independent nation back from political and economic development? The poem does not answer these questions, but it underscores how the issues of authenticity and identity are not peripheral, but central to economic and political ones.

NINE CONTINENTS: A MEMOIR IN AND OUT OF CHINA, XIAOLU GUO (2017)

In her geographically and culturally expansive memoir, Xiaolu Guo explores many of the same questions taken up in Adichie's story and p'Bitek's poem. *Nine Continents* tells the extraordinary story of how, abandoned as a baby and left to grow up with her grandparents in a small fishing village on the Eastern coast of China, she made her way to Beijing to study film, immigrated to Great Britain, learned English, and eventually became a distinguished novelist, poet, and film maker. It is in many ways a singular document in literature about the emergence of transnational writing, and the transnational writer, for Guo finds writing through becoming "a wanderer, uprooted and displaced," a "nomad in both body and mind," someone for whom both the "past" and the present are "a foreign country" (1). Her engagement with art as a young girl is pivotal to the transformation she undergoes. Reunited with her parents after her grandfather's death, she grew up in poverty, but became increasingly interested in the visual arts, first in an encounter with young art students whose work she admires, and later by her own father's landscape paintings. Eventually, with a budding interest in film, she applies—and is accepted to—the Beijing Film Academy. Here, she immerses herself in the study of transnational global cinema, analyzing a range of films, including Alain Resnais' *Last Year in Marienbad* (209), D.W. Griffith's *Birth of a Nation*, and "the films of Charlie Chaplin and Buster Keaton, Vertov's *Man with a Movie Camera*,

Murnau's *Nosferatu*," and Eisenstein's *Battleship Potemkin* (210). After a stint trying to shoot a documentary about contemporary avant-garde art being produced on the outskirts of Beijing, she went on to write a novel about a young woman named Fenfang, who, much like herself, "ran away from home for Beijing and tried to become an artist" (235), followed this with a second novel, later attempted to produce a film script that would pass muster with Chinese censors, and then worked as a soap opera writer.

Finally, frustrated with her life in China, she applied for, and received, a 2002–3 Chevening Scholarship to study film and television in Great Britain. The rest of the book deals with her life in Europe, which she calls "the land of the nomads" (279). The section entitled "Arrival" recalls both the source of the book's title, and one of its central motifs. When she was five years old her grandmother took her to a Taoist Monk who made the following prediction: "The girl is a peasant warrior, she will travel the Nine Continents" (283). Both Guo's self-description as a nomad, and the book's overarching preoccupation with mobility, displacement, and a longing for elsewhere have their source in this visit. Initially, her life in London is disillusioning:

> Perhaps I was looking for great writers to meet or great books to read, but I could barely decipher a paragraph in English .... I was convinced I would find an artistic movement to be part of, something like the Beat Generation, or the Dadaists of the old Europe. Yet all I encountered were angry teenagers who screamed at me as they passed on their stolen bikes and grabbed my bag .... What an idiot I was. Now I realised there had been some truth to my own country's Communist education: the West was not milk and honey.
>
> (286)

Since this is a book about the emergence of a transnational writer and filmmaker, the stress here is on Guo's intellectual and critical disorientation. "My previous training in China was, I quickly discovered, the enemy of the style here" (289). While her Chinese school followed a Russian model borrowed from the Moscow Film School, stressing the idea of "cinema as visual poetry, divorced from the traditions of theatre and literature" (289), the British approach was influenced by documentary journalism, so the

"Auteur Cinema" that awakened her to a life in film had little currency there. She had, at the time, "no context in which to place what the film school was trying to do," especially in a world "dominated by 'consumer demand,' which was something the Beijing Film Academy wasn't so interested in" (289). The film-makers she invoked in class were thought to be part of a hopelessly passé European tradition, and when speaking of them she found herself accused of being "pretentious," and too much of an "intellectual" (289). The irony in this becomes clear to her:

> I had been illiterate until the age of eight, and now, at the age of almost thirty, I was once again illiterate. I had to learn to speak and write in another language otherwise I couldn't construct a life in the West. Identity seemed to be a pure construction—something I had only just realised.
>
> (290)

Guo's writing about identity focuses in particular on language, which is both a key to survival and to shaping a new kind of subjectivity defined by her situation as both an immigrant and an intellectual exile. Having extended her visa after finishing her scholarship, Guo is faced with making a living, but "I could only see myself making a living through writing, as I had done in China" (302). But, how to make a living as a writer in a country whose language she spoke only haltingly? And, how was she to deal with "not just the physical loneliness, but cultural and intellectual isolation" (302)? She decides, rather than enroll in language school, to teach herself how to write, and she comes up with a surprising way to do it:

> I would make an advantage out of my disadvantage. I would write a book about a Chinese woman in England struggling with the culture and language. She would compose her own personal English dictionary. The novel would be a sort of phrasebook, recording the things she did and the people she met.
>
> (303)

Guo, in effect, decides to collapse—or conflate—the worlds of the real and the fictional, to write her way out of trouble by writing a novel about a woman who writes her way out of trouble. Here

Guo touches on one of the major motifs of transnational literature, the role that writing itself can play in negotiating the economic, personal, linguistic, and cultural challenges presented by displacement, exile, and migrancy, or of being a refugee (a theme that gets written into many transnational texts, from Walcott's *Omeros* and Hemon's *The Lazarus Project*, to Díaz's *The Brief Wondrous Life of Oscar Wao*, all of which make the protagonist's work as a writer central to their treatment of displacement and identity).

This effort leads to a fascinating episode that makes the challenge of learning English as a second language dramatically concrete. Here Guo stresses the role that language plays in shaping an individual's entire conceptual framework, the way we look at and make sense of the world, but also how the language we use both embodies and reflects political ideology. "The fundamental problem with English for me was that," unlike Chinese calligraphy, in English "there is no direct connection between words and meanings" (304). In Chinese, Guo points out, the English word "sun" refers to an extreme instance of "Yang energy," which is "strong, bright, and hot," but the English word "sun" is simply made up of the letters s, u, and n (304). Guo comes to realize that, unlike Chinese, in English "visual imagination and philosophical understandings were useless" (304). Then, there is the problem of tenses. "We Chinese never modify verbs for time or person, nor do we have anything like a subjunctive mood. All tenses are in the present" (304). This problem takes her to one of her favorite books, Jack Kerouac's *On the Road*, the Chinese edition of which, of course, had no tenses. The "whole book is in the present, like a diary" (305). Locating an English edition of the novel, she discovers it is written entirely in the past tense, which leads to the following realization about temporality itself:

> Surely a stream of consciousness, if it was anything, was a vivid form of present tense! Did that mean even youth culture in the West lived in the past? Where was their now? Did the present ever exist? ... I laid down the Kerouac book and finally gave up on the idea of using only the present tense in my new, Western life.
>
> (306)

Passages like these underscore not only the concrete challenges of learning a new language. They also underscore the ways in which language is deeply interwoven with—and profoundly shapes—the ways in which we view the world, its objects, and our everyday experiences, including how we experience—and narrate—time. The kind of experience Guo describes here is another key topic in transnational literature and serves to underscore the complex relationship between language and identity, and how that, in turn, shapes our very experience of what we take to be reality. Indeed, this is one of the key values of transnational literature in an increasingly globalized world, its ability to focus on language as a crucial factor in recognizing, coming to terms with, and negotiating cultural difference. This is underscored vividly a bit later when Guo writes about the first-person plural (one of the striking things about this portion of the book is her ability to turn what could otherwise be prosaic discussions of parts of speech into penetrating analyses of cultural and even ideological differences). As she develops her facility with English she "discovered I used the first-person plural too much in my everyday speech."

> In the West, if I said "We like to eat rice," it would confuse people. They couldn't understand who this "we" was referring to. Instead, I should have said "We Chinese like to eat rice." After a few weeks, I swapped to the first-person singular, as in "I like to eat rice."
>
> (306)

However, this makes her "uncomfortable," she explains, because she had grown up in a "collective society," while the use of the first-person singular required her to think of herself as a "separate entity in a society of separate entities" (306). In China, "no one is a separate entity," but in England, "this foreign country, I had to build a world as a first person singular-urgently" (306).

Another thing Guo needs to get used to, living in London, is the multicultural makeup of its population, which is strikingly different from Beijing, where almost everyone is Chinese. Guo provides a unique perspective on both the multicultural and cosmopolitan nature of twentieth- and early twenty-first-century cities in the West, a topic discussed repeatedly in transnational fiction, from Teju Cole's exploration of the topic in *Open City*, to Zadie Smith's novelistic treatment of London (during the period Guo was living there) in *White Teeth*. Paradoxically, she writes that she feels at home "walking among all the other non-English speaking foreigners. Bengalis, Arabs, Brazilians, Spanish, Germans, French, Italians, Vietnamese and even Icelanders! At least I wasn't the only Asian face in the street" (291). Over the years—ten before she applies for a British passport—Guo slowly adjusts to shifts in the way she thinks about her own identity, first as Chinese, then as a nomad, then British (after she becomes a naturalized citizen), but finally transnational, this last a key recognition that occurs when, at the Chinese embassy in London, she applies for a Chinese visa with her British passport, is asked if she has a Chinese passport, hands it to the agent, and has it confiscated.

> From the day I lost my Chinese passport, I came to the simple revelation that nationality didn't declare who I was. I was a woman raised in China and in exile in Britain. I was a woman who wrote books and made films .... But a passport and the nationality written on its cover would never define me.
>
> (318)

From this perspective, the subtitle of Guo's book, *A Memoir In and Out of China*, takes on a double meaning. Yes, *Nine Continents* is a memoir of her life in China, and then, of her life outside of China, but, more significantly, it is the memoir of a life increasingly lived in a space that is simultaneously both in and out of China. Near the end of the book, she writes that "I had spent the last decade with one foot in each world: West and East. I couldn't say I was fully here, and I certainly wasn't fully there" (355). Never fully anywhere, her identity is not rooted in a single place or nationality, or even in the space between them. Rather, it is lived out in simultaneity, in the almost fluid space defined by the constant movement between them, as if consciousness were mobility itself. Because it leaves the reader with this intimate insight into Guo's sense of self, *Nine Continents* provides extraordinary insight not only into what it means to be a migrant or exile in our twenty-first-century world, but what it means to be a transnational writer in that world as well.

"WHEN MR. PIRZADA CAME TO DINE," JHUMPA LAHIRI (1999)

One of the most comprehensive, yet compact treatments of identity and belonging in an age of increasing transnationalism can be found in Jhumpa Lahiri's short story, "When Mr. Pirzada Came to Dine," the second story in her collection, *Interpreter of Maladies* (1999). The story is narrated in the first person by a woman named Lilia, who was a child of ten when the events she narrates took place. Lilia and her parents, who are Indian, are living in the United States and have had a man named Mr. Pirzada as a regular visitor. Although the reader is informed at the beginning of the story that the year is 1971, Mr. Pirzada is from Dacca, Pakistan, and that the country was embroiled in a civil war that led, by the end of the year, to the establishment of Bangladesh, the ten-year-old Lilia has no clue about his identity. She simply assumes, since he looks like them and eats the same food as they do that he is Indian. However, when, early in the story, she refers to him casually as "the Indian man," her father pointedly corrects her. "Mr. Pirzada is no longer considered Indian," he tells her, not "since Partition. Our country was divided. 1947 … One moment we were free and then we were sliced up … like a pie. Hindus here, Muslims there. Dacca no longer belongs to us" (25). "It made no sense to me," the grown up Lilia interjects.

> Mr. Pirzada and my parents spoke the same language, laughed at the same jokes, looked more or less the same. They ate pickled mangoes with their meals, ate rice every night for supper with their hands. Like my parents, Mr. Pirzada took off his shoes before entering a room, chewed fennel seeds after meals as a digestive … [and] drank no alcohol.
>
> (25)

Lahiri here is foregrounding two different ways to think about identity, one cultural and the other political. From the cultural point of view, in terms of all the behaviors Lilia observes, Mr. Pirzada seems Indian. However, as her father points out, identity is also a product of politics and history, what can seem at times highly arbitrary forces that, nevertheless, define national identities in ways that divide people who were formally the same. The point of departure here, of course, is that Lilia is not aware of this history, and so the story turns into a lesson about identity, which becomes a key turning point in her life. Her father leads her to a map of the world taped over his desk. On the map India is orange, but, her father points out, Pakistan is yellow, a different country, and divided in two (East and West Pakistan), with a part of India in between. Moreover, he tells her, while Mr. Pirzada is Bengali, like them, he is Muslim, not Hindu. Her father is incredulous that she has not been taught this history at school. However, his wife reminds him that Lilia was "born here," in America (which of course means that she herself is American, not Indian). In America, she "learned American history, of course, and American geography," about the Revolutionary War, and Plymouth Rock (27). "During tests we were given blank maps of the thirteen colonies, and asked to fill in names, dates, capitals. I could do it with my eyes closed" (27).

Lahiri is making at least three important points in this episode. The first, of course, is that while one's identity can be thought of in cultural terms, identity is ultimately a legal matter. One's identity is tied to the nation-state, defined by historical and political forces that are sometimes outside one's control. The second point, of course, is that identity can be a hybrid thing, one can be culturally Indian or South Asian but be either Indian, Pakistani, Bangladeshi, or American, or experience oneself as a mixture of all four. And finally, one's sense of identity is partly a function of education. Lilia learns in the story not only that Mr. Pirzada is Pakistani (and then Bangladeshi once the civil war is over), but that she is herself not only American but also Bengali and therefore shares a mixed identity with him. Her father's history lesson sparks her own interest in her own identity, which she comes to realize is shaped by a history she does not know. Later, at the school library, she is chastised by her teacher for reading a book entitled *Pakistan: A Land and Its People* when she is supposed to be working on an American history report. The point here, of course, is that, spurred by her father's history lesson, Lilia's sense of her own identity becomes complicated in extraordinarily useful ways.

Indeed, Lahiri herself has written that composing this story proved to be a "turning point" in her own life ("To Heaven Without Dying," 2000) because it was one of the stories in which she found herself attempting to "forge my own amalgamated domain" (3). Each of the words in this phrase is important, "forge" because it emphasizes this is her own, self-made construction, "amalgamated" because it means to take disparate parts and turn them into a single mass (i.e. to blend, coalesce, fuse or combine), and "domain" because it refers to a field of action or thought, a territory or realm of personal knowledge over which one has responsibility. The domain here, for Lilia, is the personal knowledge that her identity is amalgamated, a fusion of Indian, Bengali, and American, defined both by culture and the vagaries of history and politics, and something over which she can herself take responsibility. Ultimately, for Lahiri, identity involves the act of translation, making "sense of the foreign in order to survive" (4), translating what is foreign into one's own idiom, a process she sees as "an ongoing cultural one," to "preserve what it means … to be forever Indian … in a foreign and at times indifferent world" (4). "Whether I write as an American or an Indian," she concludes, "about things American or Indian or otherwise, one thing remains constant: I translate, therefore I am" (4).

Nearly all of the texts we have been exploring link identity to the pervasiveness of mutability, liminality, transitions, and porous borders in transnational experience. Each saturates the *materiality* of everyday life, including the political, historical, geographic, and cultural formations that shape transnational experience. However, those forces, as we have seen in this chapter, affect the inner lives of characters as well. Consciousness and identity mutate, transform, and move through liminal spaces and metaphorical borders. For this reason, transnational literature often presents identity in binary terms, as the challenge of having to be, for example, both Bosnian and American, Jamaican and British, Indian and American, or to resolve the tension between urban cosmopolitanism and traditional village life. To choose one side or the other, or to opt for hybridity. For this reason, the well-known concept of "double consciousness" conceptualized by the African-American sociologist, writer, and activist, W.E.B. Du Bois, is often invoked in discussions of identity (or subjectivity) in transnational literature. "It is a peculiar sensation," Du Bois writes in *The Souls of Black Folk*, this double-consciousness, this sense of always looking at one's self through the eyes of others, of measuring one's soul by the tape of a world that looks on in amused contempt and pity. One ever feels his two-ness,—an American, a Negro; two souls, two thoughts, two unreconciled strivings; two warring ideals in one dark body, whose dogged strength alone keeps it from being torn asunder.

(2)

THE SYMPATHIZER, VIET THANH NGUYEN (2015)

The "two-ness" Du Bois refers to is at the very center of Viet Thanh Nguyen's novel about the Vietnam War, *The Sympathizer*, which deals in sustained and complicated ways with the question of identity. That two-ness, of course, is most obviously embodied in the divide between North and South Vietnam, but it also registers in the ways in which Nguyen plays "democracy" off of "communism," and American culture off Vietnamese culture. However, it is also deeply embedded in the book's complicated exploration of identity—political, national, cultural, and personal. The book is written in the first-person in the form of a confession by a Vietnamese double agent, a man working at the highest echelons of the South Vietnamese military, who at the same time is spying for the North. However, the narrator is also a double agent in another sense, since he is the son of a Vietnamese woman and a French Catholic priest. Throughout the novel he refers to himself as a "bastard," a "mongrel," a "half-breed," a "métis," and "Eurasian" (20). As a mixed-race Vietnamese, he is neither Vietnamese nor European, but here is where the complex meaning of the novel's title becomes significant, because, in the war he finds himself embroiled in, and being both Vietnamese and French, he has *sympathy* for both sides—Vietnam and the West, the North and the South. After the fall of Saigon when he travels to Southern California, with the general he is both working for and spying on, that sense of sympathy extends to America as well, both its political position and its culture.

However, identity in *The Sympathizer* is also explored in the context of another binary connected to identity: authenticity versus performance. In America, the narrator gets by through performing *both* oriental inscrutability and a seemingly willing attempt to assimilate.

Out for a drink in Los Angeles with a Japanese woman he works with, he's called out for his practiced inscrutability.

> "You can talk, and that counts for a lot. But it's not just that. You're a great listener. You've mastered the inscrutable Oriental smile, sitting there nodding and wrinkling your brow sympathetically and letting people go on, thinking you're perfectly in agreement with everything they say, all without saying a word yourself."
>
> (75)

Identity here is a kind of performance, a tool of the spy trade explicitly linked to the book's preoccupation with sympathy. In another, darker passage, assimilation is also presented as a kind of performance. He and the other South Vietnamese who have made their way to Southern California find themselves

> consumed by the metastasizing cancer called assimilation and susceptible to the hypochondria of exile. In this psychosomatic condition, normal social or familial ills were diagnosed as symptoms of something fatal, with their vulnerable women and children cast as the carriers of Western contamination. Their afflicted kids were talking back, not in their native language but in a foreign tongue they were mastering faster than their fathers. As for the wives, most had been forced to find jobs, and in doing so had been transformed from the winsome lotuses the men remembered them to be.
>
> (91)

This performance of assimilation is the dark opposite of the narrator's performance of the stereotype of oriental inscrutability, which is also a kind of pathology. The complexities of the book's meditation on sympathy and sympathizing are suggested here, as are the ways in which those themes are connected to the novel's treatment of identity. As a spy for the North, the narrator is a "communist sympathizer," but he also has sympathy for the plight of the South Vietnamese he is working with. Indeed, the confession he is writing for the Commandant who has captured him on his return to Vietnam presents him as having too much sympathy for the West. "Even in this latest revision," the Commandant points out,

you quote Uncle Ho [Chi Minh] only once. This is but one symp-
tom, among many in your confession, that you prefer foreign
intellectuals and culture over our native traditions. Why is that?
I'm contaminated by the West? Exactly. That wasn't so hard to
admit, was it?

(312)

Later, the Commandant insists on the need to choose a side,
linking his problem with doing so specifically with his identity as
a bastard.

Your destiny is being a bastard, while your talent, as you say, is seeing
from two sides. You would be better off if you only saw things from
one side. The only cure for being a bastard is to take a side.

(314)

Somewhat perversely, the narrator's double identity as a *métis*
or Eurasian makes him what the novel calls a man of two
minds, someone condemned to see everything from two sides.
This is perverse in the sense that we usually think of the ability
to see things from two sides as a virtue, but in Nguyen's novel
sympathy is a kind of burden because it keeps questions open,
and identities multiple, irresolvable into a single one, which is a
problem for rigid ideologists like the Commandant. However,
this is where the novel ultimately stakes its claim. Political,
cultural, and social discord are inevitable, and questioning and
probing from multiple sides breed complex and contradictory
forms of sympathy that, while they may not produce clear
resolutions, are productive for the ways in which they put cer-
tainties in question. This holds, in particular, for the novel's
take on identity. In the final analysis, Du Bois' concept of
double-consciousness, especially in an age of increasing globalization and mobility, seems more the norm. However, the
binary notion of consciousness (or identity) being simply double
gets complicated, as we have seen, in many transnational texts,
where the overlaps between tradition and modernity, home and
away, and multiple national cultures produce the need to
manage a constant, fluid, simultaneous experience of multiplicity and decenteredness.

SELECTED POEMS, LOUISE BENNETT (1983)

Texts like *The Sympathizer* make it clear that the topic of identity is not just a psychological or social one, but rather, is deeply embedded in history and politics. Helal certainly makes this point in her hybrid book, as Mao does in her poetry. Taken together, the writers discussed in this chapter draw on a range of writerly discourses—fiction, poetry, non-fiction, journalism, and history— in order to explore identity. One last, illuminating example is the brilliant, idiosyncratic Jamaican poet, Louise Bennett. Bennett was born in Kingston, Jamaica in 1919. As a transnational writer, she wove her study of Jamaican folklore and patois into a long career as a journalist, poet, radio, TV, and stage performer in Jamaica, Britain, and the United States. Her poetry is rooted in Jamaican culture, and is connected to an oral tradition steeped in creole and dialect, but it is attuned as well to the multinational and multicultural makeup of the nation, and committed to an analysis of a range of aesthetic, formal, cultural, and political issues related to national identity, class, color, and migration.

"A Merica," for example, begins by calling attention to the number of Jamaican families that have migrated to the United States, and pauses to ask

> Ah wonder is what fault dem fine
> Wid po li Jamaica
> Meck everybody dah lif-up
> An go a Merica?

And in a following stanza:

> Some a go weh fi vacation,
> Some a go we fi tun 'high',
> Some a fo fi edication,
> But de whole a dem a fly!
> Me ask meself warra matter,
> Me ask meself wha meck
> Is tidal wave or earthquake or
> Is storm dem dah expec?

While Bennett herself spent years abroad, this poem is openly skeptical of those who are leaving the country, whether for a vacation, an education, or for economic reasons. Another poem on this topic, "Back to Africa," questions the desire of Jamaicans to return to this ancestral homeland given the complexity of their ties to a range of other races and ethnicities. The poem is addressed to a fictional Miss Mattie, and reads in part

> Back to Africa, Miss Mattie
>
> ...
>
> Me know she dat yuh great great great
> Granma was African,
> But Mattie, doan yuh great great great
> Granpa was Englishman
> Den yuh great granmodder fader
> By yuh fader side was Jew?
> An yuh grampa by yuh modder side
> Was Frenchie parlez-vous?
> But de balance a yuh family,
> Yuh whole generation,
> Oonoo all bawn dung a Bun Grung—
> Oonoo all is Jamaican!

For Bennett—as we earlier saw was the case for the Caribbean-born Caryl Phillips—the hybrid, syncretic nature of Jamaican identity is more important than any particular aspect of that identity, which is, ultimately, not African (or English, Jewish, or French) but Jamaican. The poem ends with a series of stanzas about the futility of going back to a place from which you were never from. According to Miss Mattie's logic, that she ought to migrate to Africa because "between yuh an de Africans/Is great resemblance," the speaker notes that "all dem blue-yeye/White American/Who-for great granpa was Englishman/Mus go back to Englan," and she follows this by underscoring the complexities that would follow:

> What a debil of a bump-an-bore,
> Rig-jig an palam-pam
> Ef de whole worl start fi go back
> Whe dem great grampa come from!

The poem ends by suggesting Miss Mattie ought to feel free to travel, but she shouldn't tell anyone that she's going back to Africa because it is her home land when her homeland is actually right here in Jamaica.

While the speaker of "Back to Africa" is openly skeptical of people like Miss Mattie who are tempted to abandon their actual—and deeply syncretic—homeland of Jamaica for the ideal of a purely African one, she takes delight elsewhere in what cultural critics call colonization in reverse, the temptation in the age of decolonization for formerly colonized people to immigrate to the metropolitan centers of their former colonizers, thus disrupting the demographic, and cultural "purity" of those centers in a way that duplicates the effects of their own colonization. This is a complex topic which gets a much fuller treatment in novels like Zadie Smith's *White Teeth*, but Bennett's poem, "Colonization in Reverse," lays out this dynamic with both clarity and humor, and in an admirably condensed way. The poem, also addressed to Miss Mattie, begins:

> What a joyful news, Miss Mattie;
> Ah feel like me heart twine burs—
> Jamaica people colonizing
> Englan in reverse.

Here, England, not Africa, is the "motherlan," and colonization in reverse promises to "tun history upside dung ... Fi immigrate an populate/De seat a de Empire" (107). The speaker's delight in the ironies of this historical reversal is clear, especially in the final stanza:

> What a devilment a Englan!
> Dem face war an brave de worse;
> But ah wonderin how dem gwine stan
> Colonizin in reverse

Notwithstanding the speaker's obvious delight in this reversal, however, the poem has a steady undercurrent of satire that connects it to the kind of skepticism we observed in "Back to Africa." "Everybody future plan/Is fi get a big time job," however, "when dem catch a Englan/An start play dem different role/Some will settle down to work/An some will settle fi de dole." The poem ends with a handful of stanzas about a "Miss Jane," who is tempted to simply live off the "dole," and would rather "stay pon Aunt Fan couch/An read love-story book."

"Colonization in Reverse" was written in 1966, four years after Jamaica gained its independence from Great Britain, and at a time when immigration to England was accelerating dramatically. What is most striking about the poem, of course, is not that it registers the drama surrounding the influx of immigrants to England, but the fact that Bennett frames it in the context of colonization. She is one of the first to recognize—and explore in her poetry—the irony that colonization is a two-way street, that the transformation of indigenous cultures by colonizing nations is about, in the age of decolonization, to be matched by the transformation of colonial nations by a wave of immigrants not only from the Caribbean, but from Africa and South Asia as well. This development marks a new phase in the history of colonialism, the reversal of a historical flow which had previously been one way. The reverberations of this reversal are central to the subject matter of transnational literature which, as we have seen, is deeply engaged with the complex ripple effects of both colonialism and globalization. Indeed, the contemporary immigration crisis in both Europe and the United States, treated in Erpenbeck's, Habila's, and Hamid's novels, and the rise of conservative nationalist movements in both places aimed at preserving the so-called purity of European and American culture, are rooted in the kind of reverse colonization Bennett explores in her poem.

Poems like "A Merica," "Back to Africa," and "Colonization in Reverse" are also deeply interested in the nation as well, concerned as they are with the question of what it means to be Jamaican. While the poems we have already discussed have mostly to do with the relations between identity and place (is Jamaica the "motherland," or England, and what does it mean for Jamaican identity to be transplanted to America?), others explore the relationship between identity, national belonging, and race. "Him Deh Yah," for example, is about the sense of racial solidarity and uplift that sweeps Jamaica when the African-American singer, Paul Robeson comes to perform there. The speaker, rejoicing in his arrival, exclaims "Lawd, what a sight fi cure sore yeye!/Lawd, what a tale fi tell! ... Real-real live, what a ting!/Him gwine fi bow, him gwine fi smile/An den him gwine fi sing!" It is not so much the simple fact of Robeson singing in Jamaica that is the poem's focus, but rather, the transformative effect it has on his audience:

> An when him done, de clappin an
> De Cheerin from de crowd!
> An every nayga head swell, every
> Nayga heart feel proud!
> Proud a de man, de singer, an
> Lawd, a tenkful to yuh
> Dat when we feel proud a him race
> Dat race is fi-we too!

The key point, for the speaker, is the shared sense of racial power and solidarity experienced at Robeson's performance, the fact that the audience's pride in Robeson can transfer to themselves. Here we can begin to see what, decades later, scholars will come to see as the expression of a shared identity among those who belong not to a nation, but to a vast African Diaspora. Indeed, one of the things about Bennett's poems that makes them transnational, beyond the fact that they draw on her own experiences in Jamaica, England, and the United States, is this recognition—and celebration—of an African Diasporic identity.

Other poems by Bennett, as we have already seen, stress the mixed racial makeup of Jamaicans. "Pass fi White," for example, is about the light-skinned daughter of the speaker's friend, Miss Jane, who has gone to study in America. While "she fail her exam," she is "passin dere fi white ... She couldn pass tru college/So she try fi pass fi white." She "passin wid her work-mate-dem/She passin wid her boss,/An a nice white bwoy she love dah gwan/Wid her like seh she pass!" Where Jane sent her daughter to work on her "edication," she's learned more about "complexion" and the vagaries of the color line, that race is less biological than performative, "For plenty copper-colour gal/Deh home yah dah play white."

What makes Bennett's poetry transnational? Like Caryl Phillips, she focuses attention on the multinational, multiracial character of Jamaican identity, its hybridity. She stresses Jamaica's colonial relationship to England, its population's roots in Africa, the pull of American culture in her people, and the imperative that Jamaicans must negotiate their identity—personal and national—within the intersectionality of these disparate elements, all related to the geopolitical forces of colonialism, decolonization, and globalization. Jamaican culture, in her poetry, emerges in the tension between national and transnational sources of identity. That tension is embodied in many of the poems discussed above. Bennett's poetry, moreover, is self-conscious about its transnationality, melding a modernist poetics with Jamaican patois to produce a dramatically distinct poetic language. It is worth noting that this poetic language runs risks, for while it foregrounds everyday speech with its use of Jamaican patois, it opens itself up to the criticism that it reinforces stereotypes of black people as uneducated and unable to speak proper English and, perhaps more seriously, that especially in its performance it devolves into a kind of self-parody, criticisms that had been made earlier of African-American writers like Zora Neale Hurston, and entertainers like Louis Armstrong.

The transnationality of Bennett's poetry is also rooted in her interest in issues related to decolonization, which she often treats with irony and skepticism, as we saw in our discussion of "Colonization in Reverse." This attitude is present, as well, in "Jamaica Elevate," a poetic meditation on Jamaica's quick rise as an independent nation, and which is laced both with humor and skepticism. Written in the wake of Jamaica's independence from the United Kingdom in 1962, it's speaker observes that "So much tings happen so fas an quick," a referendum, an election, and then independence, that "Me head still feel giddy." The poem goes on to reference Jamaica's new place in the international community:

We tun Independent Nation
In de Commonwealth of Nations
From de folks of high careers;
We go Consuls and Ambassadors
An Ministers and Senators
Dah rub shoulder an dip mout
Eena heavy world affairs.

The poem goes on to reference examples of Jamaica's rise as a nation and its entrance into the international community: it has an army, a stadium, banks, a national anthem, and a governor general. It has a delegation at the U.N., membership in the Organization of American States, and dutifully tells Russia "we don't like dem" and "we meck Merica know/We is behine dem." The tone of the poem registers misgivings about the pretensions involved in this nation-building, but it seems genuinely taken with the fact that Jamaica has a ruler, a Governor-General, who actually looks like a real Jamaican. The new Governor General looks exactly like a man the speaker knows, "jus like one a we own fambly,/De very same complexion ... So yuh see how we progressin," how "Jamaica elevate." The stress here, in the final analysis, is on the achievement of self-rule, the dramatic fact that the black son of a former slave (Sir Clifford Campbell) has replaced the British Governor General (Sir Kenneth Blackburn).

The general interest in Bennett's poetry in the relationship between the local and the global, the tension between a personal or cultural identity conceived as indigenous and one shaped by Westernization, is, as we have already seen, a common one in transnational literature. It is linked to the broader interest in history that characterizes nearly all of the texts we have been discussing. The borders between past and present are shadowy in each of them. Perhaps more importantly, the past helps to shape the present, and the very question of which events from the past count as history, and whose interests that choice benefits, are put front-and-center. Past and present intersect in Tokarczuk's *Flights* in myriad ways, both for the characters within the stories she tells, and in the book's shift between different historical periods. Cole's *Open City*, as we shall soon see in more detail, is relentlessly focused on both dominant and marginalized histories—and the tension between them—and on its narrator's struggle to "find the line that connected me" to the historical "palimpsest" that is Manhattan (59). And, of course, the histories of India, Bangladesh, South Africa, Chicago, Western and Eastern Europe, the Middle East, Africa, China, and Vietnam are front-and-center in the texts we have discussed by Ghosh, Lahiri, Gordimer, Hemon, Erpenbeck, Habila, Helal, Mao, and Nguyen. In the next chapter, we take a closer look at some literary works in which history as both fact and idea is treated in ways that underscore the complexity of its importance for transnational literature.

FURTHER READING

Desai, Kiran. *The Inheritance of Loss* (New York: Atlantic Monthly Press, 2006).
Mda, Zakes. *The Heart of Redness* (New York: Farrar, Straus and Giroux, 2000).
Okigbo, Christopher. *Collected Poems* (Portsmouth: Heinemann, 1986).
Pal, Anuvab. *Chaos Theory* (India: Pan Macmillan, 2012).
Smith, Zadie. *White Teeth* (New York: Random House, 2000).

REFERENCES

Adichie, Chimamanda Ngozi. "The Danger of a Single Story." TED Talk, 2009. Retrieved at https://www.ted.com/talks/chimamanda_ngozi_adichie_the_danger_of_a_single_story.

Adichie, Chimamanda Ngozi. "Jumping Monkey Hill," in *The Thing Around Your Neck* (New York: Knopf, 2009).

Bennett, Louise. "A Merica," in *Selected Poems: Louise Bennett* (Kingston: Sangster's Book Stores, 1983).

Bennett, Louise. "Back to Africa," in *Selected Poems: Louise Bennett* (Kingston: Sangster's Book Stores, 1983).

Bennett, Louise "Colonization in Reverse," in *Selected Poems: Louise Bennett* (Kingston: Sangster's Book Stores, 1983).

Bennett, Louise. "Him Deh Yah," in *Selected Poems: Louise Bennett* (Kingston: Sangster's Book Stores, 1983).

Bennett, Louise. "Jamaica Elevate," in *Selected Poems: Louise Bennett* (Kingston: Sangster's Book Stores, 1983).

Bennett, Louise. "Pass fi White," in *Selected Poems: Louise Bennett* (Kingston: Sangster's Book Stores, 1983).

Bitek, Okot p.'. *Song of Lawino & Song of Ocol* (Portsmouth: Heinemann, 1966).

Du Bois, W.E.B. *The Souls of Black Folk* (New York: Penguin, 1996).

Guo, Xiaolu. *Nine Continents: A Memoir In and Out of China* (New York: Grove Atlantic, 2017).

Lahiri, Jhumpa. "When Mr. Pirzada Came to Dine," in *The Interpreter of Maladies* (New York: Houghton Mifflin Harcourt, 1999).

Lahiri, Jhumpa. "To Heaven Without Dying," in *Feed Magazine*, July 24, 2000.

Mda, Zakes. *The Heart of Redness* (New York: Farrar, Straus and Giroux, 2000).

Nguyen, Viet Thanh. *The Sympathizer* (New York: Grove Press, 2015).

HISTORY

Because it is the product of a long and complex set of intersecting social, cultural, economic and political developments that converged dramatically in the last decades of the twentieth century, transnational literature is deeply engaged with history. Most prominently, with the critical exploration of a range of key events broadly related to empire, colonization, modernity, and decolonization. However, it is also focused on thinking critically about the *idea* of history—who shapes its narratives and who controls what counts as history in the first place. Literature with a self-consciously transnational scope deploys the resources of fiction, poetry, and drama to explore critically, challenge, and in some senses rewrite, the historical record, using the literary imagination to call attention to the importance of history in shaping human identity, belonging, and the politics that govern nation–state relations.

It is important to stress here that such texts are not simply historical novels, poems, and plays in the narrow sense of the word, developing their plots out of historical rather than wholly imagined or fictional circumstances. They are works that explore history itself as both a concept and a historical construction. That is, they often develop a sustained meditation on the nature and function of history, stressing its importance while at the same time exploring its constructed and often ideological character. History emerges in many transnational texts as a useful instrument for remembering the past but also for shaping the present as well, something key to thinking about the history of colonization and shaping the processes of decolonization at all levels. History gets treated in many of these texts less as a set of fixed facts than discursively, as both argument and ideology, and many of the texts embrace magical realist approaches to deal with the uncanny nature of historical memory. Taking its point of departure from critics of historicism such as Hayden White, many transnational texts (and the critics who write about them) are interested in how the literary resources of historiography are used to wield power, all of which comes under the rubric of what White called metahistory – historical thinking about historical thinking (see *Metahistory: The Historical Imagination in Nineteenth-Century Europe*, passim). As we shall see in more detail below, such thinking is often shaped around a focus in transnational literature on writing itself, on an exploration of the intimate relationship between history, writing, textuality, and power. Sometimes, as in Junot Díaz's *The Brief Wondrous Life of Oscar Wao* (2007), this takes the form of a sustained focus on the relationship between language, writing, and power in which "history" is presented as something that is not only shaped by narrative and informed by rhetorical power, but subject to the very text we are reading in its efforts to rewrite it. At other times, as in Derek Walcott's epic poem, *Omeros* (1990), this exploration takes an even more overt shape in the foregrounding of two protagonists who are actually trying to write competing—and very different—histories of the Caribbean, one poetic and the other factual. Constructing the plot of his epic poem around not only the history of the Caribbean but an exploration of the various textual modes of its construction, Walcott is able to foreground not only the importance of history but also how that history is up-for-grabs and subject to being shaped in a variety of discursive modes. We will look at these texts in more details below, but we begin by returning to the important role that history plays in Teju Cole's *Open City*.

OPEN CITY, TEJU COLE (2011)

History, as we noted earlier, plays a particularly central—even exemplary—role in Teju Cole's novel. As he walks the streets of Manhattan, Julius is particularly attuned to the layers of history evoked by the places he visits. Dutch colonization, Native American displacement, the importation of African slaves, Japanese internment camps, Idi Amin's dictatorship in Uganda, the

Israeli–Palestinian conflict, and the plight of North African migrant refugees in Brussels all get extended treatment. Moreover, his own relationship to these intersecting histories becomes a key question early on in the book. It comes into focus when Julius finds himself at the site of the 9/11 World Trade Center attack, where he thinks about the layers of history buried there and his own connection to them. There was, he thinks to himself, "nothing new" about atrocity in this place, only that in the twentieth century "it is uniquely well organized, carried out with pens, train carriages, ledgers, barbed wire, work camps, gas" (58). Recalling the erasure of bodies in the 9/11 attacks, all of them vaporized except "the falling ones," he realizes that this "was not the first erasure on the site":

> Before the towers had gone up, there had been a bustling network of little streets traversing this part of town. Robinson Street, Laurens Street, College Place: all of them had been obliterated in the 1960s to make way for the Word Trade Center buildings, and all were forgotten now. Gone, too, was the old Washington Market, the active piers, the fishwives, the Christian Syrian enclave that was established here in the late 1800s. The Syrians, the Lebanese, and other people from the Levant had been pushed across the river to Brooklyn, where they'd set down roots on Atlantic Avenue and in Brooklyn Heights. And before that? What Lenape paths lay buried beneath the rubble? The site was a palimpsest, as was all the city, written, erased, rewritten. There had been communities before Columbus ever set sail, before Verrazano anchored his ships in the narrows, or the black Portuguese slave trader Esteban Gómez sailed up the Hudson; human beings had lived here, built homes, and quarreled with their neighbors long before the Dutch ever saw a business opportunity in the rich fur and timber of the island and its calm bay. Generations rushed through the eye of the needle, and I, one of the still legible crowd, entered the subway. I wanted to find the line that connected me to my own part in these stories.

(58–9)

One of the striking things about this passage is how it foregrounds the relationship between history, storytelling, and writing. A palimpsest is a piece of writing material – parchment or paper – upon which successive layers of writing have been superimposed on one another through a process of erasure and new writing. Seen through the lens of this metaphor, the island of Manhattan emerges as a kind of textual or narrative construction, a series of intersecting historical migrations of peoples and cultures written, erased, and rewritten. History gets figured here as a set of stories or narratives in which Julius himself, as a Nigerian American, is implicated. There is a line that connects him not only to the black Portuguese slave trader Gomez—and the slaves he traded—but also, by extension, to the native Lenape peoples who lived on the island, explorers like Columbus and Verrazano (an Italian who "discovered" New York Harbor), Dutch merchants, and Syrian and Lebanese migrants. His sense of belonging to a global community of displaced peoples, foregrounded first in his interactions in New York City with members of the African diaspora and in his relationship with Dr. Kaito, a Japanese professor interned during the Second World War, and later in the Brussels chapters when he meets Farouq and Khalid, refugees from North Africa, is foregrounded here because it is one of the book's central topics.

Julius' discussion with these two refugees productively complicates the relationship between history, otherness, and writing that Cole—and other transnational writers like him—is exploring. The North African immigrant he meets in Brussels, Farouq, works at an Internet café, is a former M.A. student in critical theory, and their conversation moves, in turn, from figures like Walter Benjamin, Edward Said, and Benedict Anderson to Paul de Man. These conversations quickly turn to a topic we have already touched on, the question of authenticity in postcolonial and transnational writing. Farouq is critical of the Moroccan writer Julius is reading, Tahar Ben Jelloun, who, Farouq insists, "writes out of a certain idea of Morocco. It isn't the life of people that Ben Jelloun writes about but stories that have an oriental element in them. His writing is mythmaking. It isn't connected to people's real lives" (103). There are other, more important writers, he insists, "whose work is connected with everyday life and with the history of the people" (103). Asked to recommend one such writer, Farouq mentions Mohamed Choukri's novel, *For Bread Alone* (1973).

> You see, people like Ben Jelloun have the life of a writer in exile, and this gives them a certain—here Farouq paused, struggling to find the right word—it gives them a certain *poeticity*, can I say this, in the eyes of the West. To be a writer in exile is a great thing. But what is exile now, when everyone goes and comes freely. Choukri stayed in Morocco, he lived with his people. What I like best about him is that he was an autodidact, if it is correct to use this word. He was raised on the street and taught himself to write classical Arabic, but he never left the street.

> (104)

It is important to note the distinctions Farouq is invoking here—between writing that is of the "street" and writing that indulges too much in "mythmaking," between exile and home, and between "poeticity" and realism. Authenticity, for Farouq, comes from sticking to everyday life, the streets, social realism, and the avoidance of poeticity and mythmaking. Julius quickly keys into how Farouq's critique is consistent with Edward Said's analysis of the phenomenon of Orientalism, a form of mythmaking Julius believes Western publishers of transnational literature are attracted to:

> It is always a difficult thing, isn't it? I mean resisting the orientalizing impulse. For those who don't, who will publish them? Which Western publisher wants a Moroccan, or Indian writer who isn't into oriental fantasy, or who doesn't satisfy the longing for fantasy? That's what Morocco and India are there for, after all, to be oriental.

> (104)

Farouq agrees. "This is why Said means so much to me," because he "knew that difference is never accepted. You are different, okay, but that difference is never seen as containing its own value. Difference as orientalist entertainment is allowed, but difference with its own intrinsic value, no" (104). This adds another, crucial distinction to the ones Farouq earlier invoked, between a focus in writing on cultural, ethnic, religious, national, and racial difference aimed at exoticizing it for its entertainment value, and a focus on those same differences as being intrinsically valuable, that is, having an inherent or essential value.

THE BRIEF WONDROUS LIFE OF OSCAR WAO, BY JUNOT DÍAZ (2007)

The metaphor of the palimpsest, and Julius' emphasis on how histories of conquest, travel, and migration constitute a series of stories or narratives, connect them to his own narration of the book we are reading and the history *it* recounts. In linking history, writing, and storytelling with his own novel, Cole's book is reminiscent of the moves Junot Díaz makes in his prologue to *The Brief Wondrous Life of Oscar Wao*. The prologue insists that "the New World" exists under the spell of a "curse" or "*fukú*" placed on it by conquest, colonization, and the institution of slavery (1). However, according to the narrator "the fukú ain't just ancient history, a ghost story from the past with no power to scare. In my parents' day the fukú was real as shit, something your everyday person could believe in" (2). Embodied in the mid-twentieth century Dominican dictator Rafael Leónidas Trujillo Molina, it ran in a direct line back through slavery and the historical conquest of what is now the Dominican Republic by Christopher Columbus, and forward through the U.S. government's systematic domination and exploitation of the country. Explained both in the body of the novel and in its elaborate web of documentary footnotes, these histories become a series of lessons that sketch in the geopolitical, ideological, and cultural context of the lives of its main characters.

Set up in the prologue in this way, history is presented as a shaping force one must understand in order to grasp the origins and nature of one's own condition. Crucially, that shaping is presented as the function of storytelling, of narrative and rhetorical power. A key lesson of the novel is that "history" is shaped by those who control its narrative, and that what constitutes "history" can itself be reshaped by alternative narratives. By the end of the prologue, it becomes clear that the novel we are about to read is one of those narratives, crafted to help reshape our historical understanding of the New World and thus to lift the curse or fukú. "Everybody in Santo Domingo has a fukú story knocking around in their family" (5), and "I'm sure you've guessed by now, I have a fukú story too" (6). The prologue ends by introducing the concept of what the narrator calls a "zafa" or a "counterspell": "as I write these words I wonder if this book ain't a zafa of sorts. My very own counterspell" (7). Here a familiar kind of postmodern self-reflexivity is given a historical and political inflection. The meta-fictional and the metahistorical are linked together to form an argument about the power of writing to help undo the effects of actual historical forces.

OMEROS, DEREK WALCOTT (1990)

In texts like Díaz's and Cole's, writing gets foregrounded as a kind of redemptive act that engages, foregrounds, and resists transnational histories linked to such things as travel, migration, colonization, decolonization, and globalization. We can observe this same dynamic at play in Derek Walcott's book-length poem about the Caribbean, *Omeros*. Walcott's choice of the form of the classical Western epic for his poem has elicited criticism, especially from postcolonial commentators, who in general view his poetry as too Eurocentric, overly influenced by a Western poetic canon and the humanism it is associated with. However, *Omeros* is actually carefully designed to explore such criticism. Indeed, it is a central element in the poem's larger engagement with writing, which is featured by having the protagonist, "Walcott," attempting to use the resources of the epic to write a poem about the Caribbean, a project that is pointedly juxtaposed to the efforts of another key character in the poem, the British expatriate, Colonel Plunkett, who is at the same time trying to write a straightforward, objective history of the Caribbean. To the extent this double narrative structures the poem, *Omeros* is less a poem about the Caribbean and more a poem about writing about the Caribbean.

"Walcott" (the character in the poem, that is) understands Caribbean poetry as a highly syncretic, hybrid practice, based on "improvisation," "invention," and "imitation" ("The Caribbean: Culture or Mimicry?," 55). Much like Caribbean identity itself, Caribbean poetry must draw on African, European, and indigenous practices. In this regard, "Walcott" is invested in the same positive notion of culture as contamination we saw articulated later by Appiah. There are, in this regard, no pure or authentic origins for Caribbean poetry (a point we earlier saw stressed regarding literature in general by Caryl Phillips). Well aware of the drawbacks of using a Western epic mode to write about the Caribbean, "Walcott" ends up criticizing the poem he is writing for relying too much on "Greek manure" (271). A kind of gumbo of Greek classicism, myth, history, and poetic metaphor, "Walcott" worries that it misses capturing the essence of the island (much like Farouq worried about the poeticity of some postcolonial writing). So, it is certainly the case that "Walcott's" poem relies on epic parallels, but Walcott has him do this in part to question their legitimacy and effects. And this self-reflexivity about poetry and authenticity is enriched by the poem's tracking of Plunkett's history of the island, so that *Omeros* sustains a lucid examination of the value of both a highly subjective, poetic approach to writing about the Caribbean, and an empirical one, though the whole point is to question the binary distinction between these two modes of writing, since "Walcott's" poem is deeply historical, and Plunkett's history emerges, in part, out of his own poetic imagination. Thus, the two categories of transnational writing Julius and Farouq discuss are put in tension with one another in Walcott's poem. Plunkett's empirical history is ostensibly impartial and based on research, and thus aligns with the kind of realism Farouq endorses, while "Walcott's" poem is saturated with metaphor and symbolism, relying on Homeric parallels that link it to the mythmaking and poeticity he criticizes. However, over the course of the poem the two forms intersect and blur into one another. Plunkett's ostensibly historical narrative is in fact shaped by his erotic desire for one of the island women and is thus informed by a kind of romantic mythology, while "Walcott" becomes increasingly cynical about his over reliance on what he dismisses as "Greek manure" (271), a kind of mash-up of history, poetic metaphor, and myth. Plunkett has to reconcile the historical thrust of his narrative with the emotion and mythology that drives it, while "Walcott" has to come to terms with the important role of history in the poem he is writing.

Another approach associated with the historical perspective of transnational literature is the choice many authors make to rewrite the historical record from a different point of view, one that offers an alternative to the official record or gives a voice to those marginalized by it. By revising dominant, entrenched narratives, transnational literature expands the range of stories that count as literature, and it greatly diversifies the voices that speak in and through the stories it tells. How this process happens is vividly described by the Nigerian writer, Chimamanda Ngozi Adichie, in her TED Talk, "The Danger of the Single Story." When Adichie began reading at the age of four, all she had available were American and British books for children. Not surprisingly, when she began to write, at the age of seven, she wrote "exactly the kinds of stories I was reading."

> All my characters were white and blue-eyed. They played in the snow. They ate apples. And they talked a lot about the weather, how lovely it was that the sun had come out, now this despite the fact that I lived in Nigeria. I'd never been outside of Nigeria. We didn't have snow. We ate mangoes. We never talked about the weather because there was no need to. My characters always drank a lot of ginger beer because the characters in the British books I read drank ginger beer. Never mind that I had no idea what ginger beer was …. Because all I had read were books in which characters were foreign I had become convinced that, by their very nature, books had to have foreigners in them, and had to be about things with which I could not personally identify.

Things only changed for Adichie when she discovered books by African writers, books set in Africa about Africans. Although hard to find, reading African authors like Chinua Achebe and Camara Laye led Adichie to experience "a mental shift in my perception of literature. I realized that people like me, girls with skin the color of chocolate, whose kinky hair could not form pony tails, could also exist in literature. I started to write about things I recognized." Reading only British and American books, she points out, had an "unintended consequence: I did not realize that people like me could exist in literature."

The formative experience Adichie recounts is absolutely central to the rise of transnational literature, and it underscores how, with writers like her finding a voice and a place in the business of storytelling, literature in the last decades of the twentieth century, and the first decades of the twenty-first century, became richer, more diverse, and more complex. Not only did the geographic scope of contemporary literature explode, but whole new motifs came into focus as the stories of formerly silenced generations began to intersect and cross-pollinate. As the cultural and historical perspectives from which stories were told began to diversify and proliferate, the voices of the colonized, the dispossessed, and the marginalized, those whose languages, cultures, and belief systems had been actively suppressed, began to move into the foreground. As the last few decades of the twentieth century unfolded, and because of writers like Adichie, literature became localized for readers in surprising new places, and, perhaps more importantly, history was turned inside out as new voices revisited old stories (about things like "exploration," the "new world," "manifest destiny," and "civilizing the natives"), which began to be told from the other side.

"THE HEADSTRONG HISTORIAN," CHIMAMANDA NGOZI ADICHIE (2009)

Perhaps nowhere is this strategy clearer than in Adichie's "The Headstrong Historian." Positioned strategically as the concluding story of her collection, *The Thing Around Your Neck* (2009), "The Headstrong Historian" covers in remarkably concise fashion the historical sweep of colonialism and decolonization in Nigeria from the late nineteenth century to the early 1970s. It begins with an evocation of tribal life, and then charts in succession the arrival of European traders and missionaries, the establishment of judicial, economic, political, religious, and educational institutions devoted to colonial administration, and, finally, the development of a postcolonial consciousness in a character named Grace (her given tribal name, which she takes back at the end of the story, is Afamefuna). In the early sections of the story, Grace's grandmother, Nwamgba, reluctantly allows her son, Anikwenwa (Grace's future father), to be educated at a Christian missionary school so that he can learn English and help her in court to defend her rights to property left to her by her dead husband. Instead, Anikwenwa converts to Christianity and becomes thoroughly Westernized, taking the name Michael. As he systematically rejects the food, customs, traditions, and beliefs of his native culture, his mother "felt her son slipping away from her ... Ngwamgba knew that her son now inhabited a mental space that was foreign to her" (211).

Adichie shapes the final section of the story in such a way that Grace's education as a historian enacts a kind of ritual undoing of her father's colonization. In school, she is put off by having to read a book entitled "The Pacification of the Primitive Tribes of Southern Nigeria" (215), and later, as a schoolteacher, is moved by stories she hears from people about "the destruction of their village years before by the white men's gun" (216). Later, in college, Adichie writes that Grace changes her major from chemistry to history after hearing the story of "the eminent Mr. Gboyega, a chocolate-skinned Nigerian, educated in London, distinguished expert on the history of the British Empire," who "had resigned in disgust when the West African Examinations Council began talking of adding African history to the curriculum, because he was appalled that African history would even be considered a subject" (216). Grace sees in Mr. Gboyega's intellectual and cultural colonization a reflection of her father's, and begins "to rethink her father's schooling," sifting "through moldy files in archives, reimagining the lives and smells of her grandmother's world as she researches and publishes a monograph entitled 'Pacifying with Bullets: A Reclaimed History of Southern Nigeria'" (217).

Writing as an act of reclaiming, along with Adichie's decision to make her protagonist a "headstrong historian" are crucial to the whole point of her story. "Headstrong" signals, among other things, the capacity to think critically about the whole arc of her family's experience, and to push back against the forms of capitulation to Westernization represented by both her father and Mr. Gboyega. The single story she comes to resist is the story of civilization told from the Western perspective both men have absorbed. That story is countered, reversed, and undone by Grace's reclaimed history of her people. Central to this reclaiming is the assertion of her own voice in the construction of a counter-narrative that tells the story of the West's colonization of Africa from the point of view of Africans, a reclaiming through writing from an African perspective about Africa and its place in the world that is central to Adichie's own project as a writer.

THE MOOR'S ACCOUNT, LAILA LALAMI (2014)

We can see this device operating in even more explicit ways in other transnational texts in which familiar historical events are retold from the perspective of the silenced, and in so doing reclaimed to add another, missing dimension to the historical record. One example is Laila Lalami's novel, *The Moor's Account*, which narrates the harrowing story of the first Spaniards to set foot in North America from the point of view of Estebanico, a Moroccan slave who was a member of their party. Lalami's novel is a retelling of the famous account provided by the Spanish captain, Álvar Núñez Cabeza de Vaca in his 1542 *La Rélacion*. Lalami's novel reclaims de Vaca's history by retelling it in Estebanico's voice. Lalami was herself born in Rabat, Morocco in 1968. Like Adichie, her reading as a young girl was dominated by Western literature, in this case French. Her account of the effect it had on her is remarkably similar to Adichie's:

> Of course, none of the characters in these books looked or spoke like anyone I knew. In those days, in the late 1970s, nearly all of the children's literature that was available in Moroccan bookstores was still in French. The characters' names, their homes, their cities, their lives were wholly different from my own, and yet, because of my constant exposure to them, they had grown utterly familiar. These images invaded my imaginary world to such an extent that I never thought they came from an alien place. Over time, the fantasy in the books came to define normalcy, while my own reality somehow seemed foreign. Like my country, my imagination had been colonized. I began to write when I was nine years old. Unsurprisingly, the stories and poems I wrote were in French and featured characters who said things like "En garde!"
>
> ("So to Speak," *World Literature Today*, 2009)

It wasn't until Junior High School that Lalami began to read Arabic literature, first the classics and then more contemporary fiction "featuring Moroccan characters in a Moroccan setting," some featuring heroines "much like the women in my family." The great revelation here was her discovery "that the ordinary stuff of our lives was as fertile ground for fiction as any other." At the same time, she began to realize that "writing in French came at a cost; it inevitably brought with it a colonial baggage that I no longer wanted to carry." While a graduate student in linguistics at the University of California in Los Angeles, she decided to begin writing fiction. Lacking the "eloquence" to write in Arabic, she decided to try writing her stories in English, the language in which she was writing her dissertation. In time, she writes,

> I noticed the linguistic shift enabled me to approach my stories with a fresh perspective. Because English [unlike French] had not been forced upon me as a child, it seemed to give me a kind of salutary distance. The baggage that, to me, seemed inherent in the use of French to tell a Moroccan story seemed to lessen when I used English to tell the same story.

Like Afamefuna's "Reclaimed History of Southern Nigeria" in Adichie's story, *The Moor's Account* uses fiction to reclaim a part of Moroccan history left out of de Vaca's historical narrative. De Vaca and Estabanico (who came along as the slave of one of the other explorers) were part of a larger Spanish expedition headed by Pánfilo de Narváez that became stranded on the western coast of what is now Florida, near St. Petersburg. They subsequently sailed west in crude ships until they became shipwrecked near what is now Galveston, Texas. They eventually made their way on foot back to Mexico. It took them eight years. Cabeza de Vaca wrote his *Rélacion* at the direction of Spanish authorities, and it became the official record of the extraordinary journey.

Lalami's novel not only writes Estabanico back into *La Rélacion* (she gives him the Arab name, Mustafa) but counters de Vaca's story by making hers the Moor's own account, retelling the story told by de Vaca in *La Rélacion* in his own voice and thus doubling the story. In the novel's prologue, Mustafa anticipates the danger of the single story de Vaca's account will present. "I intend," he writes, "to correct details of the history that was compiled by my companions" (3). "Unlike them," he continues,

> I was never called upon to testify to the Spanish Viceroy about our journey among the Indians ... they were led to omit certain events while exaggerating others, and to suppress some details while inventing others, whereas I, who am neither beholden to Castilian men of power, nor bound by the rules of a society to which I do not belong, feel free to recount the true story of what happened to my companions and me.

(3)

In so doing, he concludes, "my countrymen will hear about my wondrous adventures and take from them what wise men should: truth in the guise of entertainment" (4).

Where de Vaca's account presents the Spaniards as heroic survivors of Indian barbarism, Mustafa's account develops a systematic critique of the Spanish treatment of the indigenous peoples they encounter. Key to this critique is Mustafa's identification with the Indians, since he is himself a victim of colonial domination and is on the journey as a slave. Indeed, the opening sections of the novel, which tell the story of his life in Morocco under Portuguese domination, are fashioned to draw a parallel with the Spanish conquest of the Americas he later witnesses. His sympathy for the plight of the Indians Narváez's group torments develops early. He smuggles food in the dark of the night to captured members of one tribe (46). Later, Mustafa begins to assert this own autonomy as the class divisions that separate the Spanish begin to give way.

> The rules and formalities that had existed on land could not be maintained on the rafts—a nobleman had to sleep beside a black-smith; a royal official was forced to share a cup of water with a carpenter … it was a reminder that all fates, including my master's, could turn upside down. And I would do whatever it took in order to right mine.
>
> (151)

The more the Spanish become dominated by, and subservient to, the native tribes they encounter, the more Mustafa's identification with them asserts itself. This shapes a growing sense of his own complicity in enforcing the very system under which he suffered as a slave: "I could not escape the thought that I had brought all of this upon myself, first by engaging in greedy trade, later by selling myself into bondage, and later yet by stealing from the Indians" (165). Throughout this part of the narrative, Lalami goes out of her way to underscore the parallels between Mustafa's enslavement and that of the Indians. "For the last few years," he writes,

> Castilian soldiers had been traveling all the way from México and forcibly removing Indians to enslave them. They had done this to

such an extent that all the southern tribes had learned to always flee
or fight them, and to never trust them.

(219)

The more self-conscious he becomes of his identification with the
Indians, the more autonomy he feels and the more he asserts his
growing power. Aptly enough, given Lalami's stress on the power
of language and the value of self-representation, Mustafa's power
emerges through his learning native languages and serving as an
interpreter and intermediary.

The whole of the narrative is structured in such a way that, as
the plight of the Spanish becomes increasingly dark, Mustafa
becomes more free, and more powerful. During his journey, he
becomes acclaimed as a healer and a storyteller, and Lalami carefully connects this development to his transition from being allied
with the Spanish conquistadors, who "had carried the disease of
empire to New Spain" (272), to working out a close identification
with the Indian tribes he encounters. However, by the end of the
journey, when what's left of the ragged band of men reach New
Spain (Mexico City) he realizes his power has evaporated. "I had
the power that came with healing," he writes, "when I spoke,
people listened. But here, in New Spain, my words did not hold
the same value" (265).

The power that comes with healing is linked to storytelling, and
this link provides an important connection between Mustafa's
narrative and Lalami's. That is, the importance for Mustafa of providing his own perspective on the journey he has undergone with
de Vaca has its parallel in the importance for Lalami of rewriting de
Vaca's account in the voice of the Moor (just as, in Adichie's story,
Afamefuna's retelling of African history parallels Adichie's own
project). During his long journey Mustafa develops fame as a healer
and supplements his use of herbal concoctions with stories. "If I
was confronted with an illness I did not recognize, I listened to the
sick man or woman and offered consolation in the guise of a long
story … a good story can heal" (231). Later, Mustafa writes that
"I had seen how a good cure, combined with just the right story
and a little showmanship, could restore anyone's spirits" (238). The
link here between storytelling, healing, and restoration helps to
inform the restorative power of both Mustafa's and Lalami's

narratives. Mustafa's narrative is restorative to the extent it revises the one de Vaca has told, especially in terms of its stress on his own identification with the Indians whom de Vaca denigrates. Hearing de Vaca tell his version of the story to the Spanish authorities in New Spain, Mustafa realizes he is transforming his account in a self-serving way:

> We had all of us told this story dozens of times to our Indian hosts, but that day Cabeza de Vaca gave it another guise. In his account, he was no longer a conqueror who had fallen for lies about a kingdom of gold; instead he was the second-in-command of a fierce but unlucky expedition to La Florida .... He had not taken on an Indian wife .... He had not depended on his companions for his survival ... now he cast himself as our leader ... I tried my best not to resent Cabeza de Vaca's account of our adventure. I told myself that he had altered some of its details because he was the one who told the story—he wanted to be its hero.
>
> (250)

In Lalami's novel, as de Vaca's version of the journey spreads it gets picked up and embellished, and is eventually used by a Spanish bishop in a way that dramatically distorts Mustafa's own experience by reinforcing the idea of the Indians as heathens who need to be civilized and pacified by the Spanish. "There was no room," in the bishop's version of Mustafa's journey, for men

> who were guilty of thefts and their silence, accomplices to pillaging, beatings, and rapes. Nor was there room ... for Indians who did not wish to be ruled by outsiders .... He, too, wanted to tell the story of our adventure in his own way.
>
> (275)

And for his own purpose:

> So the bishop wanted us to be the instruments of a greater mission: converting the Indians to Christianity without the threat of soldiers' muskets. But I was struck by the irony of his using me as a model for such a mission. What would he think of what I had really done? I had taken the Indians' medicine and made it my own. I had adopted their

> ways of dress, spoken their languages, and married one of their women. I was as far removed from the bishop's idea of a proper Christian as an Indian was.
>
> (275)

This becomes the occasion for Mustafa to stress the importance of diverse faith traditions—Christian, Muslim, and indigenous.

> Was the diversity in our beliefs, not their unity, the lesson God wanted to impart? Surely it would have been in His power to make us of one faith if that had been His wish. Now the idea that there was only one set of stories for all of mankind seemed strange to me.
>
> (276)

Of course, this is precisely where Lalami's interest in the danger of the single story merges with Adichie's. The "official account" the Spanish authorities want from de Vaca and his surviving comrades, they are told, "will be of great help as we seek to pacify the northern territories" (284). But in Mustafa's view, this is precisely the problem. The official story codified in de Vaca's "shortened and sanitized" (286) *Rélacion* ignored the Spanish mistreatment of the Indians and justified their enslavement. When Mustafa decides to tell his own version of the story, it is because he feels compelled to counter the official version—the single, and therefore dangerous story of his journey.

> I still had one thing. My story. I had journeyed through the Land of the Indians and had witnessed many things that my companions had preferred to revise, embellish, or silence. What had been changed, perverted, or left out was the heart of our history, the part that could not be explained, but could only be told. I could tell it. I could right what had been made wrong .... I would tell the truth.
>
> (296)

The pun here in the word "right" is crucial: Mustafa, having realized the healing power of storytelling over the course of his journey, can "right what had been made wrong" by writing what had been made wrong. Mustafa makes clear, in the final paragraph of the novel, that this writing/righting has to do with the multiplication of stories, his adding the truth of his version of the story to those of the others who have told it. "In this relation," he concludes,

> I tried to tell the story of what really happened when I journeyed to the heart of the continent. The servants of the Spanish empire have given a different story to their kind and their bishop .... The Indians with whom I lived for eight years, each one of them, each one of thousands, have told yet other stories. Maybe there is no true story, only imagined stories, vague reflections .... Maybe if our experiences, in all of their glorious, magnificent colors, were somehow added up, they would lead us to the blinding light of the truth.
>
> (320–1)

Lalami's novel, seen in this light, and linked to Adichie's key point in her TED Talk, embodies a key imperative in transnational literature: using the power of storytelling to complicate the danger of the single story, to add the voices, the perspectives, and the intelligence (in all sense of that word's meaning) of formerly marginalized and suppressed cultures and regions of the world to add complexity to human experience and the historical record by viewing them from new, and formerly ignored perspectives. It is important to stress, as well, that the transnational nature of Lalami's novel comes not only from the multiplicity of voices and points of view it embodies, but by the geographical sweep of Mustafa's journey as well: from Morocco and Portugal to Spain and the Atlantic, the Caribbean, Mexico, and nearly the entire sweep of what became the southern United States. In so doing it captures the fluidity, and dramatically contingent nature of national borders, whether the nation is conceived narrowly in terms of the nation-state, or more broadly in terms of cultural and religious identities—in this case Muslim, Catholic, Iberian, Moorish, and indigenous. The single and official narrative of Cabeza de Vaca's survival gets transformed in Lalami's novel into a transnational epic in which a slave is given the dominant voice.

FURTHER READING

Desai, Kiran. *The Inheritance of Loss* (New York: Atlantic Monthly Press, 2005).
Drndic, Dasa. *Trieste*, trans. Ellen Elias-Bursac (New York: Houghton Mifflin, 2014).

Evaristo, Bernardine. *The Emperor's Babe* (New York: Viking Penguin, 2002).

Rahman, Zia Haider. *In the Light of What We Know* (New York: Farrar, Straus and Giroux, 2014).

Serpell, Namwali. *The Old Drift* (New York: Hogarth, 2019).

Thien, Madeline. *Do Not Say We Have Nothing* (London: Granta, 2016).

REFERENCES

Adichie, Chimamanda Ngozi. "The Danger of a Single Story." TED Talk, 2009. Retrieved at https://www.ted.com/talks/chimamanda_ngozi_a dichie_the_danger_of_a_single_story.

Adichie, Chimamanda Ngozi. "The Headstrong Historian," in *The Thing Around Your Neck* (New York: Knopf, 2009).

Cabeza de Vaca, Álvar Núñez. *The Account: Avar Nunez Cabeza de Vaca's La Relación*. Trans. and annotated by Martin A. Favata and Jose B. Fernandez (Houston: Arte Publico Press, 1993).

Cole, Teju. *Open City* (New York: Random House, 2012).

Díaz, Junot. *The Brief Wondrous Life of Oscar Wao* (New York: Riverhead, 2007).

Lalami, Laila. "So to Speak," in *World Literature Today*, September, 2009. Retrieved at https://www.worldliteraturetoday.org/so-speak-laila-lalami

Lalami, Laila. *The Moor's Account* (New York: Pantheon, 2014).

Walcott, Derek. "The Caribbean: Culture or Mimicry." 1974. In Robert D. Hamner, ed., *Critical Perspectives on Derek Walcott* (Washington: Three Continents Press, 1993, 51–57).

Walcott, Derek. *Omeros* (New York: Farrar, Straus and Giroux, 1992).

White, Hayden. *Metahistory: The Historical Imagination in Nineteenth-Century Europe* (New York: Johns Hopkins University Press, 1973).

TRANSNATIONAL THEATER

Unlike fiction and poetry, transnational theater is complicated by the fact that plays exist as both texts and in performance. Of course, novelists and poets regularly read excerpts of their work aloud for audiences, either in the context of a book tour, or by invitation at schools, libraries, and performance spaces. However, dramatic plays are written to be performed. Each performance is to some degree a translation or interpretation of the play in its textual form, and plays travel the globe in the form both of texts and performances. Indeed, the theater where Shakespeare's plays were initially performed was called The Globe Theater. Moreover, plays, defined generally as imagined dialogue written in the form of a story or narrative, with a beginning, middle, and end, and designed to both move and instruct audiences, can take a myriad of ever-shifting (and overlapping) forms. Shakespeare's plays, for example, are traditionally divided into three categories or genres—tragedy, comedy, and history—but in practice individual plays often combine them. Moreover, elements of all three are also embodied in two other genres, opera and musicals, forms of performance that have national origins but which, like drama, have circulated transnationally both in terms of composition and performance. Opera, for example, is generally understood to have originated in Italy, but the form soon spread to other European countries and beyond, and performances of operas quickly became a transnational affair. In the West, musical theater coalesced in the late nineteenth century around the works, in England, of Gilbert and Sullivan, and in America first in vaudeville, and then in more formal works by writers and composers like George M. Cohan,

Cole Porter, and Rodgers and Hart, George Gershwin, and Noel Coward. Like opera, however, musicals (especially mega-musicals such as *A Chorus Line, Cats*, and *The Lion King*), long-ago became a global form of entertainment. The impact of globalization on drama and performance has been immense. For a more detailed discussion of this topic see Dan Rebellato's *Theater and Globalization* (2009).

While our focus in what follows is on transnational drama as it has been shaped by the relatively contemporary forces of decolonization and globalization, it is important that we keep in mind the broad historical and geographical contexts in which performance culture needs to be considered. Seen from this perspective, the field of world drama is every bit as daunting as that of world literature. For example, as Barbara Fuchs has pointed out in "No Field is an Island: Postcolonial and Transnational Approaches to Early Modern Drama" (2012), "the turn to postcolonial approaches, inaugurated by Peter Hulme, Ania Loomba, and others in the late 1980s and early 1990s, has hugely invigorated the field of Renaissance drama," turning its attention to the impact Britain's "commercial and imperial expansion" had on the treatment of "race, empire, and economics" in early modern drama, and expanding its geographical map (125).

Katherine Biers and Sharon Marcus, in their introduction to "World Literature and Global Performance," a special issue of *Nineteenth Century Theater and Film* (Winter 2014), point out that "for much of the long nineteenth century, performance was global and global culture depended as much on performance as on literature in print" (1). For this reason, the essays they collected for their special issue "demonstrate the ceaseless mobility across national borders" that "helped to define the experience of writing for, performing in and going to the theatre throughout the nineteenth century" (1).

If we look beyond the history of the Western forms discussed above, drama as both text and performance is an even more complicated affair. Modern drama in India, for example, dates from the mid-nineteenth century, and is at once "multilingual, national, and postcolonial" (Aparna Dharwadker, "India's Theatrical Modernity: Re-Theorizing Colonial, Postcolonial, and Diasporic Formations," 2011). However, it has its roots in a rich performance tradition running back to between 200 and 1700 CE. For example, Kathakali (which means "story-play"), a form of dance drama, has been a vibrant style of performance in South India since the seventeenth century, and has even more ancient roots in Hindu temple and folk drama. Moreover, a myriad of other South Asian musical and dance story forms has circulated around the world, carried first by indentured servants to places like the Caribbean, and later under the auspices of a growing South Asian diaspora to South Africa, Great Britain, and beyond. In Japan, Noh theater (noh means "talent" or "skill" in Japanese) also melds highly stylized forms of dance and drama together into a form that has existed since the fourteenth century. On the African continent, social performances have a long history that pre-dates European colonization. In both ritual and secular forms, and melding together face-painting, dance, the use of masks, drumming, and story-telling, forms of African performance, often connected to religious festivals, have had a vibrant role in African cultures, and traveled to other parts of the world with the slave trade, where they were both suppressed and hybridized as they came in contact with Western forms of performance. The extensive global development of both African and South Asian diasporas in the twentieth and twenty-first centuries has also served to spread more modern forms of theater and musical drama from both continents—influenced by the West—around the world. While it is important to distinguish between secular forms of theatrical entertainment in the conventional Western sense of the term, and those associated, as in South Asia and Africa, with spiritual or religious expression embodying a ritual function, any historical treatment of drama in a global context must necessarily embrace a broad spectrum of practices, where music, dialogue, and choreographed movement become essential in the social performance of spectacle.

Given the transnational turn in theater and drama studies in recent decades, it should not be surprising that the field has come to focus in particular on theater as what J. Ellen Gainor has called "a site for the representation of, but also the resistance to, imperialism" (Introduction to *Imperialism and Theatre*, 1995, xii). Gainor calls attention to the irony that theater and drama had heretofore been "marginalized" in transnational and postcolonial studies, given "the strategic political and cultural force of theatrical production," especially when we juxtapose the "flexibility of theatre to the limitations of printed texts" (xii). In addition to exploring drama in the context of transnational histories of colonialism and imperialism, the essays collected in *Imperialism and Theatre* also pay careful attention to how colonized cultures develop new dramatic forms in the intersection between Western and indigenous performance practices. Theater, from this perspective, is a decidedly cross-cultural practice, a point elaborated at length by Jacqueline Lo and Helen Gilbert in "Toward a Topography of Cross-Cultural Theatre Praxis" (2002). Particularly interested in theatrical encounters "between the West and 'the rest'" (32), they distinguish between multicultural, postcolonial, and intercultural theater (33). While multicultural theater can refer broadly to any dramatic work "featuring a racially mixed cast" (33), the category tends to encompass plays "that aim to promote cultural diversity, access to cultural expression, and participation in the symbolic space of national narrative" (34). Postcolonial theater is defined specifically to encompass dramatic "practices that have emerged from cultures subjected to Western imperialism" (34). Most postcolonial theater, they point out, "is driven by a political imperative to interrogate the cultural hegemony that underlies imperial systems of governance, education, social organization and representation" (34). A good example is Wole Soyinka's *A Play of Giants*, which we will discuss later in this chapter. Finally, intercultural theater, in their view, is composed of dramatic works that seek to "transcend culture-specific codification" altogether in an effort to evoke a more transnational human condition, one that focuses on "aspects of commonality rather than difference" (37).

When we consider transnational drama as a contemporary expression of many of the performative idioms discussed above, hybridized by the forces of production, circulation, reception, and transformation characteristic of globalization, there is yet another element that makes the category a complicated one, and that is its increasing circulation and embodiment in digital forms. If, as Benedict Anderson has argued in *Imagined Communities*, the rise of print culture was central to the creation of the nation, the rise of digital culture has become central to the creation of what is sometimes called the *transnation*. If communities are *imagined*, then literature in general, and theater and performance culture in particular, play a key role in shaping a transnational imaginary, a sense in which one is a citizen not just of a nation, but of the world. The point here is that, in our own time, the locus of performance culture has shifted dramatically toward the digital (a tendency that dramatically accelerated in 2020 as a result of the COVID-19 pandemic, which has closed most theater, opera, and performance venues). It is not as if dramatic texts in print form do not remain important, nor is it the case that traditional, live stage performances are no longer central to the cultural world of what we call theater. Rather, the point is that digital platforms and streaming services like YouTube, Netflix, and Amazon Prime, and a host of other, smaller services, have become new launch pads for the shaping, performance, and circulation of original dramatic material, as well as for the re-circulation of conventional stage and musical works. Streamed films and television dramas have assumed an increasingly important role as a supplement to live dramatic performances. And on all of these platforms the mix is not just international, but *trans*national, in the sense that whether we look to conventional drama, television, film, or music, styles, storylines, and languages are cross-pollinating at an extraordinary rate.

Given the limited size and scope of this book, it would be impossible to do justice in what follows to the variety and complexity of transnational drama as we have outlined it above. This is a book about transnational *literature*, and so the discussion that follows will focus on drama in its relatively conventional sense as a print medium used as the basis for staged live performance. Approached from this point of view, we will see that transnational drama uses the resources of print and performance to deal with a similar range of issues as those we have observed in the fiction and poetry we have discussed so far—colonization, enslavement, decolonization, national identity conceived as both personal and cultural, displacement, exile, migration, and diaspora, in general, the challenges involved in constructing cross-cultural, decolonized, hybrid individual and community formations in an increasingly globalized world. As with these other genres, the geographical scope of transnational drama is wide-ranging, as scholars and critics have come to pay increasing attention to both works and forms originating in formerly marginalized or ignored regions of the world, and to its treatment of the subjects enumerated above. In particular, critics pay attention to the *intertextuality* of transnational theater, how through quotation, allusion, and adaptation, it participates in what Gail Bulman in *Staging Words, Performing Worlds* (2007) has called a "unified field of exchange." Emphasizing the idea that the nation is a kind of textual formation, she stresses the transnational nature of that formation by highlighting how "the incorporation of a precursor text into a play-text can rewrite a national discourse" (16). She also stresses how dramatic works engage in the complex circulation—and recirculation—of a range of cultural forms: "other plays, narratives, paintings, songs, newspaper articles, religious texts," etc. (235). Drama becomes transnational not just because in both its textual and performative modes it travels to nations beyond those in which it is produced, but because literature also travels through intertextuality—the quotation, reference, or allusion to one work in another (a key example we have already discussed is Derek Walcott's long poem, *Omeros*, a sustained adaptation of Homer's *Odyssey*). Intertextuality is another example of drama's (indeed, all literature's) mobility. This means that drama is transnational in at least three ways: through circulation of the written text, through performance of the written text in a theatrical context, and through the kind of intertextuality Bulman is stressing.

A case in point is the history of Shakespeare in Africa. Shakespeare, of course, came to Africa along with British colonialism in the form of what Ngũgĩ wa Thiong'o, in *Decolonising the Mind* (1986), called a "cultural bomb" (3), a device of instruction used to "civilize" the "savage," to transform native Africans into British subjects (3). Ngũgĩ, for example, attended an African missionary school in Kenya in the 1950s where he was deeply immersed in Shakespeare's plays, in both performances and recitations:

> By the end of the four years, I had seen a performance of *As You Like It* in 1955, *King Henry V* in 1956, *A Midsummer Night's Dream* in 1957, and *King Lear*. And at Alliance School, we had to recite some of Shakespeare's poetry. I recall his 18th sonnet, with the line, "Shall I compare thee to a summer's day?"
>
> In my memoir, I've related a story of one of the boys who claimed that he had used the poem and managed to win the heart on one of

the girls from our neighboring school. So all of us went about, tried to recite the poem in different ways and posing different ways, you know, imagining our future conquest of girls' hearts through his poetry. I never managed to conquer any, but I do still remember the line, "Shall I compare thee to a summer's day?"

("Shakespeare in Africa" The Folger Library)

The British, of course, used Shakespeare in part to marginalize indigenous theater in Africa, which they banned. As the Nigerian playwright, Femi Osofisan explains:

theater in our tradition is very much linked to religious practices, to festivals, religious festivals. The British colonial establishment depended very much on collaboration with the Christian missions. As far as they were concerned, these traditional festivals, which were performed with gods and so on, you know, were pagan, heathenish, and so they had to be banned.

("Shakespeare in Africa," The Folger Library)

Out of this beginning, Shakespeare becomes a kind of colonizing figure in Africa, used by the British, especially in places like Nigeria and South Africa, as an instrument of cultural subordination. However, after independence, Shakespeare, in effect, undergoes a kind of decolonization, and his plays become indigenized through translation and adaptation. This happens, in particular according to Ngũgĩ and Osofisan, with respect to the plays about power and politics. As Ngũgĩ explains:

The colonial system of education tried to colonize the revolutionary Shakespeare. In the colonial system, which while thinking it was imposing Shakespeare, was actually putting Shakespeare in chains, Shakespeare was closer to our struggles in Kenya. But the colonial system of interpreting him and so on tried to tame that revolutionary implication of Shakespeare. Particularly, the fundamental struggle for power, and in all his plays, he's able to show that power changes not through the pen, as I like to think myself, but actually through the sword. Because all his plays are full of blood, they have assassinations. And that bloodiness of Shakespeare, which was tamed by the way he was presented in the colonial classroom, the implications of that way of presenting Shakespeare and taming his revolutionary spirit, had the same result as saying, "Look, we produced a Shakespeare, you've never produced Shakespeare."

("Shakespeare in Africa," The Folger Library)

Thus, as Jane Plastow, a professor of African theater puts it, under decolonization in Africa "you get a whole lot of people beginning to adapt" Shakespeare, "you get ... increasingly radical adaptations of Shakespeare," people "taking the meat of the message" and, "in a very Shakespearean way," taking stories from Shakespeare and adapting them to an African setting. "So you take the story of Julius Caesar," she continues, and "you Africanize it. You give people African names, you put African dance in ... you Africanize its form, you Africanize its name, and to varying degrees, you radically change the structure of the piece as well" ("Shakespeare in Africa," The Folger Library).

This Africanization of Shakespeare is emblematic of the mobility of drama which, in both its textual and performative forms, is fueled in particular by colonialism, decolonization, and globalization, all of which work to foster the complex forms of hybridization we earlier saw Appiah explore. As Gainor succinctly puts it, "colonial cultures generate new theatrical forms by negotiating between indigenous performance modes and imported imperial culture" (*Imperialism and Theatre*, xiii). These negotiations, it is important to note, call attention to the instrumental uses of drama. Theater is not simply performance for entertainment, or even edification. Theater is *used*, in practical terms, to accomplish a range of sometimes diametrically opposed things—the enactment of sacred spiritual ritual, the cementing of community solidarity, the colonization, domination, and transformation of a people and its culture, and resistance *to* that domination by formerly colonized people in the appropriation, adaptation, and transformation of key elements of the colonizer's culture. And of course, an Africanized Shakespeare travels as well, enacting a complex form of recirculation as Africanized productions of Shakespeare set in Africa circulate back to the former metropolitan centers of colonialism, and beyond. One striking examples is Osofisan's *Wesoo, Hamlet!* which resets the broad outlines of Shakespeare's play in the twentieth century, incorporating Yoruba rituals, songs, and performance styles.

Another is the performance during London's 2012 Globe to Globe Festival of five Shakespeare plays originating in Africa, including a production of *Julius Caesar* set in a modern African state.

The production and circulation of transnational drama have also been fueled to a significant degree, as we have already noted, by the spread of diasporic communities (African, South Asian, Caribbean, etc.). Not surprisingly, diasporic plays deal broadly (like fiction and poetry) with the question of what it means to be a diasporic subject, with the unsettling of identities and cultural practices that come with displacement, and with the complex relationship between place, home, and belonging, with how migration disrupts the sense of having a single, fixed origin. Contemporary migration and diasporic belonging, as we have already seen, is often characterized less by permanent relocation than by back-and-forth migration, regular visits back to one's home country to see parents and friends, etc. Diaspora thus becomes a kind of fluid, mobile, shifting space, a locality without a fixed geography.

Beyond Bollywood and Broadway: Plays from the South Asian Diaspora (2009) collects and briefly analyzes 11 representative plays written by South Asian diasporic writers in the United States, Canada, the United Kingdom, and South Africa. As the book's editor, Neilesh Bose explains, these plays, "written *by* and *about* South Asian diasporic people," examine key ideological, political, cultural, and personal subjects that recur among South Asia's diaspora playwrights and establish a kind of baseline for exploring the emergence of a "diasporic performance aesthetic" (2). Bose points out that

> long before the modern era's migrations of indentured laborers in the nineteenth century and middle-class professionals in the twentieth, South Asians were connected to other parts of the world by pre-modern trade routes and ancient exchanges of culture, ideas, and texts.
>
> (3)

With the advent of indentured labor in the nineteenth century, poor and working-class South Asians migrated to places like South Africa and the West Indies. After independence and partition, that demographic began to change as people from the professional middle classes began to immigrate abroad. Many made their way to Great Britain, Canada, and the United States, further broadening the geographic scope of the South Asian diaspora. However, as Bose also notes, while the phrase "South Asian Diaspora" may denote geographical locations, it "does not coherently describe the various historical, cultural, and political experiences of the peoples in all these locations" (5). In the final analysis, "South Asian" is a multinational designation, and "diaspora" has less to do with geography than it does with mobility.

Because, as we have seen throughout this book, transnational mobility produces increasingly hybridized or creolized individuals whose subjectivity is shaped by multiple linguistic, cultural, social, religious, and political forces, transnational theater often focuses, as Bose notes, "on processes of identity formation" (5). However, like fiction and poetry, it also "reflects a highly diverse set of socio-political and aesthetic concerns" (6). Two particularly important examples are Anuvab Pal's *Chaos Theory* (2002) and Jatinder Verma's *2001: A Ramayana Odyssey* (2001). In Pal's play, Sunita and Mukesh meet as young humanities students at Delhi University in the 1960s and go on to sustain a life-long friendship as they move to the United States for graduate work and eventually secure teaching positions at Harvard and Columbia. Pal (who lives in the United States) plays Mukesh's Anglophilia (he is enthusiastic about Elizabethan literature) off of Sunita's commitment to subaltern literature and culture. Built around an exploration of their experiences as elite academics in the West, the play dramatizes the postcolonial condition in a diasporic context in which Mukesh's Westernized sensibility is contrasted with Sunita's academic and class-room devotion to Indian mythology, literature, and culture. Each deal in their own way with what Bose calls "colonial modernity" (13). As Pal has put it in an interview, Mukesh "thinks there is no difference between himself and Harold Bloom" (the famous Yale literary critic), while Sunita is forced, in Bose's words, into "peddling India" until she becomes, according to Pal, "depressed" and "frustrated with academia, with having to sell one's ethnicity to get bigger grants" (12). In the end, Mukesh ends up marginalized in American academia, while Sunita decides to return to India to pursue her career.

Like Walcott in *Omeros*, Verma (based in Great Britain) relocates and rewrites a classical epic, in this case *The Ramayana*, which he puts in dialogue with the *Odyssey*. Where Pal uses the diasporic context to put India and the West in dialogue through his characters, Verma puts his two classical texts in dialogue with one another in order to explore migration and its discontents. The play features Rama and a host of characters from *The Ramayana* in dialogue with Odysseus and many prominent characters from the *Odyssey*, including a chorus. Rama counsels Odysseus, and vice versa, and much of it has to do with their relationship with women; Odysseus' with Circe and Penelope, and Rama's with Sita, which makes the relationship between gender and power an important theme in the play. A Western sense of duty gets contrasted with Rama's belief that there is such a thing as *dharma* (a cosmic law of order or correct way of living) that must be fulfilled. While the story is mainly structured along the lines of the plot of the *Odyssey*, Verma infuses the play with elements from Indian performance, especially in its dance sequences, its music, and the expressions of the chorus which are turned into Vedic chants. As they are woven together, the motif of the journey in each text is used to dramatize issues related to migration, especially the tension between home and away-from-home we earlier saw Brik speak of in Hemon's *The Lazarus Project*.

Theater in the Hispanic Caribbean is similarly rooted in an exploration of diaspora, migration, and identity. As Camilla Stevens notes in "Hispanic Caribbean Theatre on the Move: Crossing Borders, Redefining Boundaries" (*Latin American Theater Review*, 2016), it is impossible to understand theater in the region without "developing a nuanced understanding of Hispanic Caribbean migration as a diaspora composed of men and women from various nations, regions, and social backgrounds," and who "have migrated for different reasons at discrete historical junctures and who have lived the diaspora in diverse ways" (206). Nonetheless, she observes in the range of Cuban, Dominican, and Puerto Rican dramatists and performers she has studied "a long-standing transnational mode of collective belonging," a sense of diasporic identity that transcends affiliation with a particular nation (206). Like Bose, her work is marked by a dual attention to common subjects and aesthetic styles in the drama she discusses, as well as to the diversity and heterogeneity of the plays she discusses.

René Marqués' *The Oxcart* (1969), for example, set in Puerto Rico, is about a rural family so poor they are unable to pay the mortgage on their land. They move first to a slum neighborhood in San Juan, and then migrate to New York City. There they experience an erosion of their Puerto Rican identity and values, which are associated with their former rural life in Puerto Rico. *Oxcart* contrasts their commitment to stability, freedom, moral decency, and pride in labor with the materialism, mechanized labor, and crowdedness of New York city. The play's contrast between the language, customs, and values of the family's rural lives with the urban world of New York City, while a familiar literary plot, is given nuance by its engagement with the contemporary forces of globalization and its focus on postcolonial displacement and migration. Manuel Martín Junior's *Union City Thanksgiving*, about three generations of Cuban Americans who have left Castro's Cuba, also dramatizes the loss of identity that can come with migration. While the younger generation finds it relatively easy to assimilate, the older generation does not. Centered around a Thanksgiving celebration in their new home in Union City, New Jersey, the family is bound not by a connection to their national identity and the cultural world associated with it, but by the trauma of leaving Cuba. The food served, a mix of Cuban and American dishes, foregrounds transculturation. In a final example, *Ashes of Light* (2012), by Marco Antonio Rodriguez, features a group of characters who migrated from the Dominican Republic to New York City, and who long ago developed a transnational identity. While the mother lives in NYC, her son lives in Dallas. Reunited at the death of the father, the mother struggles to come to terms with her son being gay. She is confused by his passion for Shakespeare and the theater, and he finds her closed-minded and provincial. As in *Union City Thanksgiving*, generational differences are foregrounded in *Ashes of Light*, embodied in the contrast between the mother's attachment to her homeland and her son's assimilated life in Dallas.

Finally, in order to get a clear sense of how transnational drama deals critically with the colonial, neo-colonial, and geopolitical frameworks of both postcolonialism and globalization, we can turn to Wole Soyinka's *A Play of Giants* (1984). The play is set in the New York embassy of a fictional African country, Bugara, where the leaders of four fictional African countries are sitting for a group sculpture. As he explains in a note at the beginning of the play, Soyinka has specifically modelled these leaders on four African dictators. "Benefacio Gunema" is based on Macias Nguema of Equatorial Guinea, "Emperor Kasco" on Jean-Baptiste Bokassa of the Central African Republic, "General Barra Tuboum" on Mobuto Sese Seko of Zaire, and, perhaps most importantly, "Field Marshal Kamini" is based on the infamous Ugandan dictator, Idi Amin. Kamini is hosting the group and is the main character in the play. While all of these leaders think of themselves as postcolonial liberators who "have uplifted" Africans "from the degradation of centuries of conquest, slavery and dehumanization" (22), Soyinka represents this as rhetoric intended to mask the repressive, neocolonialist nature of their own regimes, which includes the systematic plunder of their countries' economic wealth. Each of these leaders is fixated on power (political, but also spiritual and sexual). As Gunema says to the other dictators, "you take power through army. You fight. You conquer .... Your method is straightforward, it has clarity" (21). Chillingly, Kasco follows up with the insistence that power has to be grabbed and is authoritarian:

> We fight, we kill, or we die .... Power comes only with the death of politics. That is why I choose to become emperor. At the moment of my coronation, I signal to the world that I transcend the intrigues and mundaneness of politics.
>
> (21)

Of course, in actuality, power is nothing if not political in Soyinka's play, and "politics" in the play are not local, or even African, but global. Soyinka drives this point home by dramatizing how these African dictators are caught not only between the power of their former colonizers, and the United Nations, but that of three superpowers, the United States, Russia, and China as well. Tuboum insists that "all the big powers make trouble" and that "only the Chinese are different," while Kamini counters that while "the Chinese are my friends" they "have no money" (43). Kasco sides with the French, while Kamini reports that "we discuss America when we eat lunch, and it give us indigestion" (44). In the middle of this discussion two Russians enter to pay tribute to the leaders on behalf of the Soviet Union, praising Tuboum in particular for

> his courageous defeat of the imperialist conspiracy launched against him in his country by neo-colonial stooges and agents who are attempting to install puppet regimes all over the continent in order to facilitate their shameless plans for the continuous exploitation of the struggling peoples of Africa,

(44)

driving home the obvious irony that each of these dictators is doing precisely the same thing. Late in the play it is announced Kamini has been overthrown in a coup, and he blames not only the United States and the Soviet Union, but the World Bank and the United Nations.

This focus on both the historical and geopolitical contexts in which African dictatorships emerged (at one point, Batey, a journalist, insists that Kamini "is a product of the economic and historical conditions of our people on the continent," that it is "colonial history which must bear full responsibility for all seeming aberrations in African leadership" [55–6]) drives home the point that though Soyinka's play is about corruption across Africa, *The Play of Giants* is meant to cast a wider net. It focuses our attention on the historical and structural elements that have shaped geopolitical and geocultural forces on a global scale, which is why the issues his play deals with ultimately intersect with the more contemporary ones discussed above. These issues are not just local or national. They are transnational.

FURTHER READING

Bose, Nielesh, ed. *Beyond Bollywood and Broadway: Plays from the South Asian Diaspora* (Bloomington: Indiana University Press, 2009)

Bulman, Gail A. *Staging Words, Performing Worlds: Intertextuality and Nation in Contemporary Latin American Theater* (Lewisburg: Bucknell University Press, 2007).

Conteh-Morgan, John, with Dominic Thomas. *New Francophone African and Caribbean Theatres* (Bloomington and Indianapolis: Indiana University Press, 2010).

Gilbert, Helen, ed. *Postcolonial Plays* (London and New York: Routledge, 2001).

Henke, Robert, and Eric Nicholson, eds. *Transnational Mobilities in Early Modern Theater* (New York: Routledge, 2014).

Reiter, Seymour. *World Theater: The Structure and Meaning of Drama* (New York: Horizon Press, 1973).

REFERENCES

Allers, Roger, and Irene Mecchi. Music Elton John, Lyrics Tim Rice. *The Lion King* (New York: New Amsterdam Theater, 1997).

Anderson, Benedict. *Imagined Communities: Reflections on the Origin and Spread of Nationalism* (London: Verso, 1986).

Biers, Katherine, and Sharon Marcus. "World Literature and Global Performance" in *Nineteenth Century Theater and Film*, 41 (2), Winter 2014.

Bogaev, Barbara. "Shakespeare in Africa." The Folger Library. Retrieved at https://www.folger.edu/shakespeare-unlimited/africa.

Bose, Neilesh. *Beyond Bollywood and Broadway: Plays from the South Asian Diaspora* (Bloomington: Indiana University Press, 2009).

Bulman, Gail. *Staging Words, Performing Worlds: Intertextuality and Nation in Contemporary Latin American Theater* (Lewisburg: Bucknell University Press, 2007).

Dharwadker, Aparna. "India's Theatrical Modernity: Re-Theorizing Colonial, Postcolonial, and Diasporic Formations," in *Theatre Journal*, 63 (3), October 2011, 425.

Fuchs, Barbara. "No Field is an Island: Postcolonial and Transnational Approaches to Early Modern Drama," in *Renaissance Drama*, 40 (1), 2012, 125–133. Available at: https://www.jstor.org/stable/41917504

Gainor, J. Ellen, ed. *Imperialism and Theatre: Essays on World Theatre, Drama and Performance* (London: Routledge, 1995).

Kirkwood, James, Michael Bennett, Nicholas Dante and Edward Kleban. *A Chorus Line: The Book of the Musical* (Lanham, MD: Applause Theatre & Cinema Books, 1994).

Lo, Jacqueline, and Helen Gilbert. "Toward a Topography of Cross-Cultural Theatre Praxis" in *The Drama Review*, 46 (3), Fall 2002, 31–53.

Martín Jr., Manuel. *Union City Thanksgiving* (1982. TS. N.p.).

Marqués, René. *The Oxcart*, translated and edited by Charles Pilditch (New York: Scribner, 1969).

Ngũgĩ wa Thiong'o. *Decolonising the Mind* (Portsmouth: Heinemann, 1986).

Osofisan, Femi. *Wesoo, Hamlet! or, The Resurrection of Hamlet (Re-reading Shakespeare's Hamlet)* (Opon Ifa Acting Editions, 2012).

Pal, Anuvab. *Chaos Theory* (India: Picador, 2002).

Rebellato, Dan. *Theater and Globalization* (New York: Red Globe Press, 2009).

Rodríguez, Marco Antonio. *Ashes of Light (La luz de un cigarillo). Dreaming the Americas Series* (NoPassport Press, 2012).

Stevens, Camilla. "Hispanic Caribbean Theatre on the Move: Crossing Borders, Redefining Boundaries," in *Latin American Theatre Review* 50 (1), Fall 2016, 205–221.

Webber, Andrew Lloyd. *Cats* (London: New London Theatre, 1981).

INDEX